MASONIC TRIVIA

AMUSEMENTS
&
CURIOSITIES

PETER CHAMPION

DEDICATION

Cmdr. George Peter Champion, USNR

Father, Brother, Companion, Sir Knight, Past Master

&

The brothers of King David's Lodge #209, F. & A. M.

San Luis Obispo, California

CONTENTS

	Acknowledgements	i
1	Introduction	1
2	Strangely Amusing Novelties	3
3	Did You Know?	18
4	Curiosities	30
5	Oops, Stuff That's Wrong	48
6	Don't Tinker With the Tiler	57
7	Clothes Make the Mason	64
8	The Circus Comes to Masonry	69
9	Birds of a Feather	82
10	Gentlemen, Cock Your Pistols	88
11	Ghosts of the Past	95
12	It's a Whole Different Game	108
13	Chips From the Quarry	113
14	The Halls of Justice	132
15	Brothers at Arms	139
16	One Day of Wonder	146
17	Disturb Not The Sleep Of Death	150
18	Not All Qualify	164
19	Unconventional	167
20	Presidents and Such	176
21	The High and The Low	191
22	Renaissance Mason	207
	Glossary	212
	Bibliography	215
	Index	219
	About the Author	223

ACKNOWLEDGMENTS

Past Master M. Robert Bettencourt, for his enthusiasm in researching the history of early San Luis Obispo Masonry and spearheading the historic restoration of King David's Lodge #209, as well as, catching my typos.

Past Master William "Bill" Berry, for his inspiring stories of Masonic lore and gifts of long out-of-print books.

To the Lodge Secretaries, Lodge historians, Lodge Officers, brothers at numberless Lodges who have preserved Masonic history and trivia in Lodge minutes and trestleboards, and to the many who put up with my emails and phone calls to verify details, my heartfelt, thanks.

My deepest appreciation to my wife Jan, our dear friend Connie Dennis, and my eldest son Peter Scott Champion for their unending hours of proofreading the numerous drafts. Any solecisms that remain are my errors, not theirs.

Happy Trails,
Peter

Cover Photo – top banner
1914 Knights Templar Easter Assembly
San Luis Obispo Commandery #27

CHAPTER 1

INTRODUCTION

Friends, Masons, Companions, lend me your ears;
We come to laugh with men, not to laugh at them,
The strange things Masons do live after them,
Their trivia is oft entombed with their bones,
Let it instead, be here in tomed.

M y profuse apologies to the Bard of Avon, William Shakespeare, a non-Mason, for paraphrasing his opening in *Julius Caesar.*

There is no end to the list of great literature that will live on in the halls of academia for millennia to come. This book is not one of them. It is a sampler of strange, curious, laughable, haunting, whimsical, and head-shaking oddities of Masonic trivia offered up for your amusement, with a ticklish dash of enlightenment. My goal is that you will chuckle while saying, "Wow, I didn't know *that!*"

Within these pages you will discover a tattooed corpse, dwarfs, giants, a hot-air balloon, a sunken submarine, a taxidermy-stuffed African man's body, the US Patent Office, ghosts, racehorses, a blood splattered Lodge Room, a fraternal mouse, a cod fish, pirates, western outlaws, a slave-trading President, an empty California Gold Rush tin-can, a broken lawnmower, and the missing skull of a Presidential candidate.

These stories are each a thread in the tapestry of Masonic history and humor gleaned from newspaper accounts, court documents, Lodge archives, monthly trestleboards, and the traditions of Freemason Lodges from around the globe.

To maximize the pleasure of non-Mason readers or to refresh the recollection of a Masonic brother who has allowed his trowel to become rusty, there is a Glossary at the back of this book that contains abbreviated definitions of some of the common Masonic terms found within these pages.

My wife enjoys knitting. There is a style of knitting socks called "Widdershins Knitting", where the socks are knitted by starting at the toe and working toward the opening at the cuff, instead of the traditional method of starting at the cuff and knitting toward the toe. In Shakespeare's time the terms "widdershins and deasil" were commonly used to mean "counter-clockwise and clockwise" respectively, but the words are not used much anymore. So it is with words within the rituals, ceremonies, trestleboards (monthly newsletters), and jargon of Freemasonry.

On a personal note, I enjoy visiting Lodges whenever I travel. Always, I meet a great bunch of gents with lots of interesting stories. I thank you for allowing me to share my experiences of fraternal goodwill and good times with you.

Happy Trails and Enjoy the Read,

Peter Champion

www.MasonicTrivia.com
Author@MasonicTrivia.com

CHAPTER 2

STRANGELY AMUSING NOVELTIES

Where to begin a chapter that starts with the words "Strangely", "Amusing", and "Novelties"? I've decided to tell you about a fish.

The Atlantic cod can grow to over six feet in length and weigh over two-hundred pounds. In the United Kingdom, cod has been the popular and favored white fish in "Fish 'n Chips" since time immemorial. It remains a traditional source of protein throughout the English Isles and Western Europe.

One day in 1847, the Lodge Tiler (a guard) at Glasgow Star Lodge #219 in Glasgow, Scotland, made his way to a local fishmonger, who sold him a freshly caught cod *"of fair size for family dinner fare"*.

When Bro. Torbet (the Tiler) opened the belly of his family's evening meal, a discovery of unprecedented surprise greeted him and gave him fodder for a Masonic "fish tale" unlike any heard before or since.

For nigh on to one-hundred sixty-five years the cod's surprise has been displayed as memorabilia at Glasgow Star Lodge, for inside Bro. Torbet's cod was a Freemason's lambskin apron.

The Lodge records are silent as to whether or not the Tiler's cod received a Masonic funeral, but prayers were said.

In 1964, Shakespeare Lodge #750 of New York, New York, sponsored Miss Zelda R. Suplee to a couples' social evening event, as their featured speaker. The topic of her presentation was not what most Freemasons expect at their Lodges. Miss Suplee was known as "The First Lady of Nudism" and her presentation was titled "Nudism and Mental Health". Shakespeare Lodge records indicate the attendance exceeded expectations. No mention was made of the evening dress code.

Operative Masons make use of many natural materials in their construction; sand, stone, clay, chalk, ash, and lime. Speculative Masons incorporated some of these materials in their lectures or illustrative portions of their Degrees.

Masonic lectures originally contained references to "pan". As the English language evolved, so did this portion of the First Degree Lecture. Masons still have the lecture, but the material is now referred to as "clay". The original meaning of pan continues to exist in the English word "hardpan".

Bro. Nugent of Potunk Masonic Lodge #1071 of Westhampton, New York, operated a local blacksmith's shop. In 1926, Bro. Howard Havens commissioned a set of officers jewels as a gift to the Lodge. Nugent forged the jewels from discarded lawnmower bushings and scrap parts. Later, the Lodge had Nugent's cutting edge artwork silver-plated.

Alpha and Omega are Greek letters that represent the Beginning and the End, like A and Zed (Zee) in the English alphabet. There may be fateful significance in these Greek letters for Dibble Lodge #109, formerly of Nevada County in California.

Dibble Lodge received its Charter in 1856 and began in the town of Alpha, California.

Dibble relocated in 1862 to Omega, California, where it ended its existence twenty years later.

Have you ever heard a Mason say, "It rains", on an otherwise sunny day? The practice comes from the early eighteenth century when Masons began using the phrase to warn other Masons that a non-Mason was present or approaching and might overhear their conversation.

The countries with the most Masons are, in descending order: 1. United States of America; 2. England; 3. Canada; 4. Australia; 5. Italy (with the exception of Stato della Città del Vaticano or the State of Vatican City, were there are none.).

It has been reported in sundry Masonic journals that a Lodge Secretary in the Midwest was presented with a custom designed officer's jewel. It reflected the change in secretarial duties over the centuries. Instead of crossed quills, his jewel was a gold plated representation of a computer keyboard.

Let's talk about curlers. Neither the purple and pink plastic ones in hair salons, nor the sweet twisted ones in donut shops, but the ones with big 42 pound or 19 kilogram stones.

In 1979, a group of Canadian curlers were on a tour of Scotland. The Canadian Curlers were also Freemasons. On January eleventh, they received a deputation from the Grand Lodge to visit Lodge Albert #448 of Lochee, Dundee, Scotland, to observe the conferral of a Degree.

Being that the sport of curling originated in Scotland, the evening could not be allowed to pass without a challenge.

According to local accounts, the two groups had a stacking of brooms (socializing with opponents and teammates) knowing they might be on keen ice in a bonspiel of "The Roaring Game" (playing on fast ice in a tournament of Curling). This may seem less than noteworthy Masonic history. But this American author has a lifelong fascination with curling, and this is the only Masonic-Curling reference I have discovered.

Reverend Josiah Henson was born into slavery in 1789. In 1829, he escaped from Maryland and made his way into Canada, where he became a Methodist preacher.

Harriet Beecher Stowe met Rev. Henson in Boston. He is widely believed to be her inspiration for *Uncle Tom's Cabin*.

In 1876, Bro. Henson published *Uncle Tom's Story of His Life: An Autobiography of the Rev. Josiah Henson*.

At the age of forty-eight, he became a militia captain of the 2nd Essex Company of Coloured Volunteers of the Canadian Army during the Rebellion of 1837. He wrote of the time in his autobiography, saying, "My company held Fort Maldon [Malden] from Christmas till the following May, and also took the schooner *Anne* and captured all it carried ... The coloured men were willing to help defend the government that had given them a home when they had fled from slavery."

Bro. Henson was a member of Mount Moriah Lodge #4, a Prince Hall Lodge in Dresden, Ontario, Canada, where he is buried. His headstone bears a Masonic Square and Compass. He was the first black gentleman to be commemorated on a Canadian postage stamp.

John Gutzon de la Mothe Borglum is world acclaimed as the artist who designed and began construction on the monumental Mount Rushmore Memorial sculpture in South Dakota's Black Hills in 1927.

Borglum was Raised a Master Mason in Howard Lodge #35 of New York City, New York, on June 19, 1904. He was

Master of the Howard Lodge for 1910 through 1911 and involved in Scottish Rite Masonry. The cornerstone to his studio near Stamford, Connecticut, was laid by the Grand Lodge of New York. He and his son, Lincoln, created a number of famous Masonic sculptures. He also designed the 1925 United States commemorative Stone Mountain half-dollar coin that depicted images of Robert E. Lee and Stonewall Jackson mounted on horseback.

The strength in the grip of the Lion's paw is an important allegory made use of in Masonic symbology, and it is the centerpiece of this story. Lodge gavels are generally made in one of three styles. The most common design is the "presidential style" or mallet that looks like the letter "T" with the striking cap shaped like a barrel. The "common gavel" style looks like a mason's working hammer with a wedge shaped edge on one side and a flat edge on the other. The Master's gavel is still called a hammer in some Irish Lodges. The third style is the "setting maul" that resembles a church hand-bell or miniature "speed bag" used in the pugilistic training of boxers.

When Borglum was Master of Howard Lodge, he crafted a setting maul styled gavel for his use. The striking part that would normally resemble the miniature boxing speed bag, was cast in bronze and sculpted in the shape of a lion's paw, with the claws grasping a chunk of stone. The stone shard came from the "Wailing Wall" of King Solomon's Temple in Jerusalem. The handle was pure white.

Borglum's unique Lion's Paw Gavel is currently on display among the property of the Lodge of Antiquity #11 in Brentwood, New York.

When Philanthropic Lodge #304 was founded in 1794, the brethren met in a pub in Kirkgate Leeds called the Crown

Inn. The selection of a pub as a meeting place was by necessity, not by choice; it was the only hall available. The first meeting was less than auspicious, only a handful of men drinking ale in a room illuminated by smoky tallow candles.

Apparently the smoking candles were not the only smoke to have caused a problem among the brothers. A mere three months after the first gathering, cigars and pipes were banned during their meetings. The Lodge minutes reflect that any brother wishing to smoke was compelled to retire from the pub and indulge his habit on the cobbled street.

The brothers put up with the poor quality tallow tapers for two years before footing the extra money for the Senior Warden to purchase cleaner burning wax candles.

It took seventy-one years before the Lodge was able to move from conducting meetings in a pub. In 1865, they took occupancy of a building that still stands behind the Leed's Town Hall at 25 Great George Street. The Lodge sold that "non-pub" building in 1893. After several changes of ownership, it currently houses "The Irish Pub".

The officers of the Grand Orient of Egypt wore clothing similar in style to the Grand Lodge of England, but with two significant differences. The colors in Egypt were "Thistle and Sea Green" instead of the "Blue and Gold" of England, and the officers' jewels were supplemented with gold stars on their collars. The more stars, the higher their rank in the Lodge.

It would be logical to assume that the tools of operative masonry selected by Freemasons for their lectures would encompass all the essential implements to be found in any stonemason's tool chest, but two are missing. In modern American Freemasonry, there is no metal chisel, nor its accompanying mallet. This was not always the case.

These tools are explained in the Mark Master Degree of York Rite Masonry. At one time, this degree was part of the Craft Lodge ritual in America. By the time an early American brother was Raised to the Sublime Degree of Master Mason, he would have received the Mallet and Chisel Lectures.

Freemasons in different countries include some form of recognition to their country's flag or sovereign during the opening of their meetings. But, this practice is not an official part of the Masonic ritual. The reason is simple and easily understood when examining United States Masonry and the Pledge of Allegiance to "Old Glory". Masonic ritual has existed for centuries, but the official use of our Pledge is younger than this author.

The "Pledge" was first written by Francis Bellamy, a socialist and preacher who had been fired from his Baptist church for "his socialist heterodoxy" in 1891.

Bellamy wrote a pledge that was published in the September 8, 1892, issue of *The Youth's Companion* that read:

"I Pledge allegiance to my Flag and the Republic for which it stands; one nation indivisible, with liberty and justice for all."

During World War Two, on June 22, 1942, the 77th Congress made the Pledge official. They changed the words "my flag" to "the flag of the United States of America".

It was not until June 14, 1954, that President Eisenhower signed a provision adding the words "under God".

Sir Arthur Conan Doyle, the acclaimed inventor of Consulting Detective Sherlock Holmes and his partner, Dr. John Watson, was a Freemason. Bro. Doyle was Initiated an Entered Apprentice Mason on January 26, 1887, in Phoenix Lodge #257 of Portsmouth, England, Passed to Fellowcraft on

February 23, 1887, and Raised a Master Mason on March 23, 1887.

There are three references to Freemasonry in Dr. Watson's accounts of Sherlockian mysteries: A "Freemason ... watch-charm" in *The Adventure of the Norwood Builder*, a "Freemasonry ... arc and compass breastpin" in *The Red Head*, and a "tie pin" in *The Adventure of the Retired Colourman*.

In *Valley of Fear*, Doyle mentions the "Eminent Order of Freemen", "The Ancient Order of Freeman ... Lodge No. 29, Chicago", and "The Society of Freemen" who "... spread their rule of fear over the great and rich district which was for so long a period haunted by their terrible presence." (Dear Reader, remember that Doyle wrote fiction.)

In January 1849, California was the land of "Gold Rush" opportunities, and men were traveling west to stake their claims at fortune. A handful of Freemasons who joined the westward migration brought with them Charters from eastern Grand Lodges to form local Lodges. A provisional Lodge was formed in Sacramento when a group of these brothers rented the third floor of "The Red House" on "J" street for $750 a month. At the time the Masons moved in, the building was unfinished, and its only other occupant was a hardware store on the main floor at ground level. Red House sported a sign painted in bold block letters along the lengths of the side and front of the building advertising, "GROCERIES & MINERS SUPPLIES & HARDWARE".

The four groups of Masons bearing Charters from Connecticut, the District of Columbia, Maryland, and New Hampshire met at Red House on April 17 - 18, 1850, to form the Grand Lodge of California. They elected Jonathan D. Stevenson as the first Grand Master. Stevenson had been commissioned a Colonel by President Polk in Baja during the brief Mexican War. He was also a lawyer and lucrative California real estate developer.

By the time of this April election, the construction on Red House was completed, and the building was fully occupied. The landlord had filled the second floor with a group of tenants whose services required no billboard advertising in order to garner customers. The stairway from the ground floor to the third floor was an open affair, it was therefore necessary for the Masons to pass by the second floor occupants in order to reach the level of the Lodge room.

The Masonic brothers were upset with the new business being conducted on the second floor and immediately moved from Red House. As a future Grand Master commented, the occupants on the second floor were disqualified from becoming Masons, both on account of "their gender and morals". These business women belonged to that ancient sorority euphemistically known as the "Sisters of the Scarlett Solicitors", who wore not white aprons, but black laced garters.

There have been two Grand Lodges for the State of California. The first was the "Grand Lodge of Ancient York Masons for the State of California".

California Lodge #13 of San Francisco refused to recognize this first Grand Lodge because delegates from "three regularly Chartered Lodges" had not been present at its formation. They argued that of the four Lodges present (Benicia City Lodge U.D. [Under Dispensation], Connecticut Lodge #75 of Sacramento, New Jersey Lodge U.D. of Sacramento, and Western Star Lodge #98 of Benton City) only Connecticut and Western Star were regular Lodges.

Under Dispensation Lodges hold meetings only at the good will of the sitting Grand Master. In addition, Benicia City Lodge was operating under the clandestine authority of the Louisiana Grand Lodge of Ancient York Masons.

The eventual result was the April 1850 meeting at the infamous Red House. Charles Gilman, who was the Past Grand

Master of both New Hampshire and Maryland, declined the offered position of Grand Master and recommended his law partner, Colonel Jonathon D. Stevenson.

The six Lodges were renumbered to reflect the new Grand Lodge of California. The numbers were intended to represent the order in which they each held their first meeting. Lodge #1 should have been assigned to Western Star, but the new Grand Master was a member of the San Francisco Lodge.

The order assigned was: California Lodge #13 became Lodge #1, Western Star #98 became Lodge #2, Connecticut Lodge #75 became Lodge #3, New Jersey Lodge became Lodge #4, Benicia Lodge became Lodge #5, and Sutter Lodge of Sacramento became Lodge #6.

Israelitic Masonic Lodges display three volumes of sacred law upon their altars as an invitation and evidence that all brothers are truly welcome; the Hebrew Bible, the Christian Bible, and the Moslem Koran.

Every Freemason goes through three rituals to become a Master Mason: he is Initiated an Entered Apprentice, Passed to Fellowcraft, and Raised to the Sublime Degree of Master Mason. Fate was not so simple for Philip Withal Shepheard.

An Englishman from birth in Plymouth in 1813, Shepheard became a seafaring youth and was so engaged throughout his early Masonic travels.

A French Lodge Initiated him in a cave near Alexandria, Egypt, before he sailed to Jamaica.

The English Lodge Masons of Kingston, Jamaica, accepted his petition for the Fellowcraft Degree. However, his French ritual was so "foreign" to them that they required him to be Initiated a second time.

The winds changed before they could Pass him to Fellowcraft, and he was again under taut canvas.

Making port in New York, Shepheard again attempted to be Passed. This time, the Empire State brothers found both his English and the French work too alien for them, and they Initiated him yet a third time.

Many tides rose and fell before he arrived in Rio de Janeiro, where the brothers of St. John's Lodge #73 saw fit to Pass the persistent man into the Second Degree.

By the time Bro. Shepheard reached San Francisco in 1849, he was Captain of the *Arkansas*. Needless to say, his jumble of French, English, American, and Portuguese rituals was the likes of which they had never heard, and they decided he needed to be Passed again in due form.

Eventually, he was Raised a Master Mason in an unrecorded California Lodge in early 1851.

With both his wanderlust traveling and Masonic traveling behind him, Bro. Shepheard settled in California. On October 23, 1853, he was appointed by the Deputy Grand Master the Right Worshipful Townsend Thomas as the first Worshipful Master of the newly Chartered Mount Moriah Lodge #44.

W.Bro. Shepheard served as both a judge in San Francisco and Grand Treasurer of the Grand Chapter of Royal Arch Masons until his death in 1865.

Bernard Pierre Mangam's Masonic journey was much shorter than W.Bro. Shepheard's. Emperor Napoleon III appointed him Grand Master of the Grand Orient of France. Mangam served in the post from 1862 to 1865, even though Mangam had never been a Freemason.

The Grand Lodges in France, England, and America have had numerous differences in practice and ritual over the centuries. The English and Americans regularly met in taverns and pubs. The French forbade that practice in 1777. That same year, the French began issuing new passwords every six months. The English and Americans have maintained the ancient passwords without change for three centuries. The French have allowed women Masons. The Americans have the coed Eastern Star, but forbid distaff membership in their Craft Lodges. The English have three "ruffians" in their Third Degree ritual. The French have "assassins" and the number has varied from three.

A fraternity is a brotherhood. The 2011 officers of Modesto Masonic Lodge #206 are a unique example of this principle. For the only recorded time in California Masonic history, three brothers held the three "Pedestal" offices (equivalent to President, First Vice-President, and Second Vice-President); Nicholas Kellner as the Worshipful Master, Eric Kellner as the Senior Warden, and Michael Kellner as the Junior Warden.

One would assume the Master was the eldest brother, but it was actually Nicholas, the baby of the three at thirty-four, who commanded that post, or pedestal.

Satirist H.L. Menchen once called the dry Martini, "the only American invention as perfect as the sonnet." So what is this perfect cocktail's connection to Masonry? Was the French bartender at Lotta's Fountain who created the beverage in 1874 a Freemason?

Nobody knows if Julio Richelieu was a Mason, but it is doubtful, because California barkeepers were excluded from becoming Freemasons. What is known is that miners and prospectors would come into his Martinez, California, saloon with old leather tobacco pouches filled with gold dust and nuggets seeking something out of the ordinary. Richelieu would serve up his new invention, a "Martinez Special". Frontier dental hygiene was not what it is today. Between missing a few teeth and a couple of drinks in their blood streams, the miners seldom pronounced the final "Z", calling the drink a "Martini". Richelieu's invention of dry gin and vermouth with lemon peel twist and a San Joaquin Valley green olive garnish lives on far beyond the borders of that dusty mining town. His saloon is no more; in its stead are a parking lot and a brass Historical Marker on "Masonic Street".

One of the largest Masonic parades in America was held on Thanksgiving 1920 in Detroit, Michigan. It was held both in memory of brethren lost during the First World War and for the groundbreaking of the new Masonic Temple.

Twenty thousand Masons and Knights Templar participated in the march. Palestine Lodge #357 had over 2000 marchers. Ionic Lodge #474 had over 1500 men on foot.

The officers wore white gloves and the aprons of their office. Other Masons wore white aprons and white gloves. Knights Templar were in full regalia, with many on horseback.

It is a good thing the brothers of one Canadian Lodge learned to count their numbers in grade school.

Within their 1997 membership, Zion Lodge #77 in Kerrisdale, of what was once Point Grey, but is now in Vancouver, British Columbia, Canada, had sixty brothers. These sixty brothers almost exactly represented each year of age for the sixty ages from thirty to ninety.

Catalina Island Lodge #524 first met as the Catalina Circle Club in 1919, with members representing numerous Southern California Masonic Lodges. The Catalina Circle Club petitioned the Grand Lodge of California in 1922 and was granted a Charter. They met in Tremont Hall, in Avalon on

Catalina Island, until 1989. That year, they "moved ashore" to the mainland in Temecula, California.

Catalina was the only Lodge in California to include among its list of officers an "Official Clock Winder".

Bro. Cyrus E. Hull was Initiated on March 23, 1852, in Hampton Masonic Lodge of Springfield, Massachusetts. He maintained current dues throughout the remaining eighty-three years and nine days of his life, making him the American Mason with the longest provable membership.

Rev. Canon William Henry Cooper did a lot of traveling, both Masonic and intercontinental. As an Anglican missionary for the Society for the Propagation of the Gospel in Foreign Parts, Rev. Cooper was in New Zealand in 1870. He moved his ministry to Australia in 1877. In 1882, he changed location to Canada under the Archdeacons of Saskatchewan. He returned to England in 1891, where he was a founder of the charitable Hostel of St. Luke. He was its Secretary from 1891 to 1894 and a resident at his death on April 13, 1909. Throughout his life, he was an avid lecturer on behalf of the S.P.G., a Fellow of the Royal Geographical Society, and an extraordinary Mason, always affiliating with the local Lodge.

W. Bro. Canon Cooper was a member of seventeen Masonic Lodges on three continents. He was the founding Worshipful Master of three of those Lodges.

Nathaniel Butler was Governor of Bermuda, in 1620, when he commissioned construction of the stylish "Italianate" government State House.

The mortar used to cement the local limestone blocks in place was an amalgam of "donkey-wheel ground lime" mixed with sea turtle oil. Hopefully, this didn't lead to the sea turtles becoming endangered.

Butler mistakenly believed Bermuda's climate would be the same as Italy's because of similar latitudes. He was unaware of the problems a flat-roofed structure would have on a subtropical island. The damage from seasonal storms to the State House resulted in major roof design modifications being installed less than a decade later.

During the American Revolution, a group of Bermudians supportive of the colonialists stole British gunpowder stored in the State House and smuggled it to George Washington's army.

In 1815, Bermuda's Parliament outgrew the village of St. George and transferred their Capital to the town of Hamilton. Many brothers changed their affiliation to a Lodge in Hamilton. The remaining brethren of Lodge St. George #200 of the Grand Lodge of Scotland found the move to be a blessing in disguise. Fortuitously for the Masons, the government's move vacated the historic two-story State House building. The Masons negotiated an affordable fixed annual rent *in perpetuity*, for the use of the building as their Lodge Hall. In an annual April pageant appropriate to the pomp of a royal wedding, the Brethren of St. George wear their Masonic regalia as they march from their Lodge to King's Square. In the Square near the replica dunking-stool and pillory stocks, they greet the arrival of the Governor in his magnificent horse-drawn landau carriage accompanied by the Mayor of St. George. Amid the pageantry and splendor of a military parade, complete with rifle salutes, the Worshipful Master holds forth a polished silver salver topped with a velvet pillow bearing the Lodge's yearly payment, negotiated nearly two centuries ago, not a payment in silver or gold, but a single black peppercorn.

CHAPTER 3

DID YOU KNOW?

Thirty-nine states offer at least one style of specialty license plates related to Freemasonry. In thirty-six states, the plates are adorned with a Square and Compass logo, with the accompanying caption FREEMASON, MASONIC FAMILY, MASONIC FRATERNITY, MASTER MASON, or BLUE LODGE on the plate.

Eleven states offer a license plate referencing Prince Hall Masonry. Eleven states have offered specialty plates for Shriners. Seven states have had plates for Eastern Star. Maryland has offered a Scottish Rite license plate.

Manitoba, Ontario, New Zealand, and Western Australia have also issued special plates for Freemasons.

As special as these special plates may seem, it is humbling to realize that Mississippi has issued an Elvis plate, and Rhode Island issued a plate depicting Mr. Potato Head.

In the Presidential campaign of 1948, the National ballots carried a slate of four Freemasons: the Democratic Party candidate was Harry Truman of Belton Lodge #450 in Missouri, the Republican Party candidate was Thomas E. Dewey of Kane Lodge #454 in New York, the States' Rights Democratic Party (Dixiecrats) candidate was J. Strom Thurmond of Concordia Lodge #50 in South Carolina, and the Progressive Party candidate was Henry A. Wallace of Capital Lodge #110 in Iowa.

If the Internet had existed in 1948, what would the conspiracy bloggers have made of them apples?

Parthenon Lodge #1101 of New York City, New York, was charted on July 2, 1929, as "The First Greek Lodge in the United States." It is the only Lodge in America to have conducted proceedings and lectures in Greek. *Opa!*

When Worshipful Master Stark was installed at the first meeting of Esmeralda Lodge #6 of Aurora, Nevada, on October 10, 1863, the Mineral County town was only three years old and had seventeen silver mills. Today, it is a crumbing ghost town. The ornate officers' jewels worn during the 1863 installation ceremony were donated by San Francisco jeweler John W. Tucker. The jewels were crafted from silver refined from the local Aurora Mining Co. mine.

Marge Mi was landscaping her flower bed in Stafford County, Virginia, in September 2006, when she discovered a gold ring in a pile of river rock. The ring was a 14th Degree Scottish Rite ring inscribed with the name Frank John C. (Clinton) Zeising and the date of "Feb. 11, 1921".

Bro. Zeising was born in San Francisco in 1890, became a 33rd Degree Mason in San Francisco, and died in San

Francisco in 1968. Nobody knows how his ring found its way from California's Golden Gate to Marge's garden gate.

Mickey Mouse was never a Freemason, but he was a member of DeMolay, a Masonic youth organization. Mickey's creator, Walt Disney, was active in DeMolay in his youth and inducted into the DeMolay Legion of Honor. In 1931, Mickey appeared in a series of strips sporting the DeMolay insignia. The strips and individual drawings of Mickey with the insignia were signed by Walt himself. The only organization Mickey was ever identified with in any comic strip was the DeMolay.

The Pencil is one of the working tools of a Master Mason in England, but not in the United States.

President Ulysses Simpson Grant never became a Freemason, although he mentioned that he had thought about petitioning for membership. Grant's father, Jesse, belonged to Bethel Masonic Lodge #61 of Bethel, Ohio.

President Grant's birth name was not Ulysses Simpson. His given name was of Masonic origin, Hiram.

President Taft sent two small blocks of oak to the Grand Lodge of Ohio. The wood came from the USS *Constitution, Old Iron Sides*. At Taft's suggestion, a gavel was made "from that part of the deck once red with heroes' blood". Taft was a member of Kilwinning Lodge #356 in Cincinnati, Ohio.

Dr. Anderson, in his *Constitutions of 1738,* goes into detail with descriptions of the Four Old Lodges that formed the first Grand Lodge of London and Westminster in 1717. As he listed them, they were: The Goose and Gridiron Ale House in St. Paul's; The Crown Ale House in Parker's Lane; The Apple-Tree Tavern in Charles Street, Covent Garden; The Rummer and Grapes Tavern in Channel Row, Westminster.

These early Lodges had all adopted the names of the ale-houses where they met.

In Louisiana of the 1800s, Masons possessing Charters under the Grand Orient in France, practiced a *Louveteau Adoption. Leouveteau* was the French form of Lewis, meaning a son of a Mason. This obsolete French practice was a form of baptism when a son was born, whereby the Lodge pledged to care for the boy until he reached the age of majority. The practice was deemed "irregular", meaning prohibited, in English and American Lodges.

On Galveston Island, in the Gulf off the coast of Texas, a Masonic groom and his bride can be wed in a "Masonic Wedding". Masonic wedding ceremonies have also been administered in Puerto Rico, Greece, Turkey, France, and the Netherlands.

On November 25, 1863, a wedding took place in the Lodge Room of Lessing Lodge #557 of Chicago, under special dispensation of the Grand Lodge of Illinois. The groom was William Heineman and his bride, Miss Katie Gross. The minister and service were German Lutheran. Neither the groom nor anyone in the wedding party was a Freemason. So, why was the ceremony held in the Lodge?

Lessing Lodge sat on the site of the groom's original family homestead, and the groom was a well-respected Chicago businessman.

Five years after his wedding, Heineman joined Lessing Lodge and became its Worshipful Master for the years of 1877 through 1880.

The early trade guilds and liveries of operative stonemasons, from which modern Freemasonry sprang, were not always composed of enlightened and genteel gentlemen.

These guilds were called societies in France and had an odd practice called "toping". Toping consisted of members from opposing societies engaging in brawling, fighting, and dueling. One of the bloodiest such topings occurred in 1730 between the Sons of Jacques and Soubise Society and the Sons of Solomon Society. The bloodshed was so atrocious that military force was called in to restore the peace and remove the dead.

Another of the practices in these guilds was that of "howling". This practice came in handy after that bloody toping of 1730, when the surviving brethren would "howl" or wail during the funerals of deceased members of their society.

Why is a wind blowing due East or West called a "Mason's Wind"?

Legend says that during the construction of the Temple of King Solomon, the craftsmen relished a breeze that blew due East or West, as it could pass through the Temple cooling workers as they pursued their labors.

Theodore Fitz Randolph was the son of a US Congressman. Theodore went on to become president of the Morris & Essex Railroad Company, Governor of New Jersey, a United States Senator from 1875 to 1881, and Worshipful Master of Varick Lodge #31 of Jersey City, New Jersey. One of his political views that evoked much controversy was his belief that the major economic problems of the country arose from minting different denominations of coins out of different metals; copper, zinc, nickel, silver, and gold. He believed in mono-metalism or the minting of all coins from the same metal.

Among his less successful ventures was that of promoting his invention of a steam powered typewriter.

Grand Lodges have the final say in approving or rejecting the name of a Lodge. Rejections are few, but one rejection in 1898, by the Grand Lodge of Idaho, mashed the hopes of a there being a "Lodge of the Potato".

Most people assume that the name of Anchor Lodge #273 in Compton, California, was chosen for its symbolism of Christianity. During the second century the cross gained in popularity as the primary symbol of Christianity, but it didn't fully surpass the anchor until the Battle of Milvian Bridge when Constantine defeated Manutius in October of 312. But, Anchor Lodge got its name in 1884 for a different reason.

The early proposed name of Alfalfa Lodge was considered, naming it for the local agricultural cash crop. Saner heads prevailed, and the Lodge was named for a local business owned by the sibling of one of the Lodge brethren. The name of the business? The Anchor Cheese Factory.

Södermanland is in the south-eastern part of Sweden between Lake Mälaren and the Baltic Sea. In 1778, the Duke of Södermanland rewrote the Sweden Masonic Ritual in its entirety.

In 1809, he created an additional Eleventh Degree of the Swedish Rite, naming it "The Civil Order of Charles XIII" in honor of the King. The new Degree was appropriately named, because in 1809, the Duke was better known by his new title of Charles XIII, King of Sweden.

It took over 600,000 red bricks to build Mount Hermon Lodge #118 in Asheville, North Carolina. The brass door knobs on the second floor bear the design of a Square and Compass surrounded by a large letter "G". The brass knobs on the third and fourth floors bear the double-eagle design of Scottish Rite.

When construction began in 1913, it cost the Lodge $1,042 to excavate for a basement. It is a good thing the brethren spent that money. The basement is where they installed the recreational bowling alley and pool tables.

Lee Lodge #209 in Waynesboro, Virginia, was founded December 12, 1866, and named with the permission of General Robert E. Lee. This Lodge in the beautiful Shenandoah Valley is the only Masonic fraternity to which General Lee granted permission to use his name.

Football fans scratched their heads from 2006 to 2009 as Quarterback Brett Favre retired, then didn't retire, then did retire, then changed his mind yet again.

Russian Freemasons under Czar Alexander I probably felt the same befuddlement as to the status of their beloved fraternity.

Alexander outlawed Freemasonry in 1801. In 1803, he joined the Freemasons and rescinded his decree, only to outlaw the fraternity once again in 1822.

Under the Common Law of England in Sir William Blackstone's time, the term "Time Immemorial" referred to events occurring since July 6, 1189, or the beginning of the reign of *Cœur de Lion* or Richard the Lionheart.

In heraldry, it refers to events occurring since the Battle of Hastings on October 14, 1066.

In general use, it means time since records, tradition, or the memory of men. This meaning is usually construed in Freemasonry to reference events after 1717, with the formation of the Grand Lodge in England.

The term "Primitive Freemasonry" is also called "Antediluvian Masonry". Within the fraternity, it refers to Masonic legends that pre-date Noah and the Great Flood.

The first recorded occasion of a formal Freemason ceremony for the laying and dedication of a cornerstone was on August 2, 1738, in Edinburgh, Scotland, for a new Royal Infirmary.

Many of the 56,545 people killed in the Buchenwald concentration camp of Nazi Germany were men arrested for being Freemasons. Even behind the barbed wire, the emaciated survivors managed to conduct Masonic funeral services for deceased brothers.

Beginning with the Neoclassical Revival in 1893, architects designed entablatures using columns and capitals from the three classical orders of Doric, Ionic, and Corinthian styles to cover the Worshipful Master's and Chaplain's chairs in the East of the Lodge Room.

Another popular style was faux porticos that resembled the *galilees* (arched covered doorways) of classic cathedrals where penitents would enter the sanctuary.

Before these classical structures were built into Masonic Lodges, a *baldachin* or canopy was draped above the Oriental Chair where the Worshipful Master sat, which gave the East a ... well, an Oriental look.

Why are blue blazers with brass buttons referred to as "Lodge Jackets"?

The practice alludes back to 1730, when legs of drafting compasses were made of brass (yellow) with steel tips (blue). Descriptions of Masters and officers wearing "Yellow jackets and blue breeches" are common, and pictures exist of Irish Lodges from the 1800s with Masons wearing this attire.

Tailed-coats and breeches would seem out-of-place in a contemporary lodge, and a blue blazer with yellow brass buttons serves as a subtle reminder of a historic fashion statement.

Four national leaders have been members of Federal Lodge #1 in Washington, D.C., President Teddy Roosevelt, President Franklin Delano Roosevelt, President Andrew Jackson, and President William Potter Ross.

I can hear you asking, "Who was President Ross?" Ross was President and Principal Chief of the Cherokee Nation in 1866 and 1874.

"Gosh dang nabbit!" doesn't sound like a curse that would be uttered from the lips of a crusading Templar Knight, and it wasn't. So, what did a Sir Knight say when accidentally whacking his thumb with a midieval mallet?

In the sixteenth century, the phrase *"By the Peacock!"* was referred to as the "Templar's Curse" in both England on the east side of the Atlantic and in New England on the west side. This author's Quaker grandmother was occasioned to use the words when small ears were present.

Why by the peacock? In early Christianity, the peacock represented the Trinity. The Templars were noted for their battle-cry of *"Dieu le Veut"* or "God Wills It" during the crusades.

While on the topic of Knights Templar, their effigies on ancient tombs depict some of them with their legs crossed and some with their legs parallel. Masonic tradition indicates that as early as 1177, Knights were buried with their legs crossed if they had actually fought in the Holy Lands in a Crusade, otherwise, their legs were laid straight and parallel.

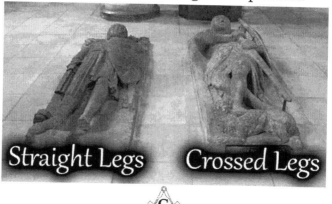

Part of the Masonic ritual in every jurisdiction involves taking a roll of twelve Fellowcraft laborers from King Solomon's Temple. It would seem a simple matter for all the Grand Lodges to agree on the names of these twelve historic workmen, but they don't. In fact there are seventy-two names that are used in one or more states.

Aarom, Abner, Abraham, Adonijah, Adoniram, Ahab, Ahinadah, Ahishar, Aholiab, Ammishaddai, Amos, Amuel, Asa, Asher, Azariah, Azzur, Belshazzar, Benjamin, Bezaleel, Caleb, Dan, Daniel, Dekar, Elijah, Elisha, Ephraim, Ezra, Gad,

Gerber, Haggai, Hesed, Hezekiah, Hosea, Iddo, Ideon, Ira, Isaiah, Issachar, Jacob, Jarman, Jedidiah, Jeremiah, Jeroboam, Jeshua, Jethro, Joab, Joseph, Josephus, Joshua, Judah, Levi, Mica, Naphtali, Nathan, Nehemiah, Obadiah, Obed, Ruben Rueben, Satolkin, Shallum, Shimei, Simeon, Talmun, Uri, Zabud, Zadok, Zebulun, Zedekiah, Zephaniah, Zerbal, and Zimry.

Even states using the same names will have them called in different orders during the roll call; and you thought it was difficult to remember the names of the seven dwarfs.

The brothers of Ione Lodge #80 in the gold mining region of Amador County of California, found themselves in a pickle. The brethren couldn't access the second-story Lodge Room from the ground floor. The solution was a stairway next door inside the building owned by the Native Sons of the Golden West, Ione Parlor #33.

There must have been something about Freemasonry that attracted early American automotive manufacturers. Henry Ford, Walter P. Chrysler, Ranson E. Olds of Oldsmobile and REO fame, George W. Mason of Nash-Rambler, and John North Willys of JEEP fame were Freemasons all.

Mencius was a Chinese Confucian style philosopher in the Fourth Century. Mencius believed the basic nature of man was good and emphasized the concept of "zhi" or wisdom. Among the lessons attributed to Mencius, two stand out for Freemasons.

"A man should abstain from doing unto others what he would not they should do unto him, and this is called the principle of acting on the square."

"A master stonemason, in teaching his apprentices, makes use of the compasses and the square. He who is engaged in the pursuit of zhi must make use of the compasses and square."

In the early 1900s, Roman Catholics were banned from "communing" with Freemasons. This did not dissuade the Masonic fraternity of Boulder, Colorado, from opening their doors to the local Catholic diocese to conduct church fairs and fundraisers inside their Lodge.

Freemason Street in Norfolk, Virginia, was constructed in 1762 and was named because there was a Masonic Hall upon the street. It is the oldest street in America named Freemason or Masonic.

Freemason Bob Burns was a popular radio host and comedian during the 1930s. He was a member of Van Buren Masonic Lodge #6 in Van Buren, Arkansas. After leaving vaudeville, his radio shows featured skits with a faked hillbilly family, where he played an instrument he invented using a length of tubing from a moonshine still and a whiskey funnel. It was part trombone, part string flute, and part kazoo.

In 1941, the US Army issued a new anti-tank recoilless shoulder fired rocket propelled grenade to troops in North Africa. The weapon was the M9A1. The troops thought it looked like the hillbilly instrument of Bro. Burns and gave it the name he invented for his instrument, the Bazooka.

CHAPTER 4

CURIOSITIES

What would it cost to build King Solomon's Temple today? In First Chronicles chapter 22, David explains to his son, Solomon, that he is to build a grand temple to the Lord. In verse 14, David explains that he has set aside funds for the building. "I have prepared for the house of the Lord a hundred thousand talents of gold, and a thousand-thousand talents of silver; and of brass and iron without weight, for it is in abundance. Timber also and stone have I prepared and thou mayest add thereto."

The Hebrews of ancient Palestine had adopted the Babylonian measure of a talent. The Babylonian talent of gold or silver weighted 30.3 kilograms (67 pounds).

There are 32.15 Troy ounces per kilogram which results in 974.145 Troy ounces per talent for Solomon.

In the first quarter of 2011, gold was worth $1,427 per Troy ounce and silver was worth $49.45 per Troy ounce.

Before Solomon assigned the first stonemason to the quarries, he had at his disposal the modern day equivalent worth of 1.4 trillion dollars in gold and 48.171 billion dollars in silver.

Chapter 29 of First Chronicles informs us that Solomon received an additional 3,000 talents of gold from Ophir along with 7,000 talents of silver. From the princes he received an additional 5,000 talents of gold and 10,000 darics along with 18,000 talents of brass, 100,000 talents of iron, and a treasure of precious stones. The Queen of Sheba sent 120 talents of gold and precious stones, and Solomon received an additional 666 talents of gold every year.

Give or take a few hundred billion, Solomon had the equivalent of one and a half trillion United States 2011 dollars to spend on his temple, and this was before a progressive income tax with the IRS taking a cut.

Question: the portrait of what Freemason has appeared on more United States stamps than any other person?

If you thought of George Washington, you would be wrong. The correct answer is De Witt Clinton.

Clinton was a United States Senator from New York, Mayor of New York City, and Governor of New York. He was Grand Master of New York in 1806, Grand Priest of New York in 1816, and Grand Commander of the New York Knights Templar in 1814. He was Governor of New York during the imbroglio of "The Morgan Affair". More importantly for philatelists, he was Governor when the Erie Canal was completed in 1825.

The fiftieth anniversary of the opening of the Erie Canal occurred in 1875, and a stamp design was prepared by the Bureau of Engraving and Printing depicting Bro. Clinton. For what many at the time believed to be political reasons, the design was not used for the planned postage stamp.

Three years later, the government needed to print a new taxpaid revenue stamp to be placed on packages of cigarettes. The oval portrait of Clinton fit the center design and was inserted. Different stamps were made for each denomination as measured by the size of cigarette packaging: 5, 8, 10, 12, 20, 24, 40, 50, 80, and 100 cigarettes. Each year a different series number was issued in various sizes. In total, over six hundred different designs were used. Every package of both Class A and Class B cigarettes from 1878 through June 30, 1959, bore a stamp carrying the original picture of W. Bro. De Witt Clinton.

Liquor, booze, hooch, or whatever label one applies to these spirits; this potent potable is the cause of differing standards among nearly every Grand Lodge.

Arkansas, Georgia, and North Carolina state that the owning or operating of a business that sells or distributes this beverage is a disqualification from membership.

Arizona, Kentucky, Louisiana, Montana, and Oklahoma prohibit it in the Lodge building.

Florida, New Jersey, Virginia, and Wisconsin prohibit it in the Lodge building except for officially sanctioned Table Lodges. Virginia expressly permits its use in the Lodge for the conferring of Knights Templar Orders.

Six states have a rather unusual disqualification as regards the manufacturing, selling, or distribution of alcoholic beverages. Namely, Alabama, Iowa, Kansas, Missouri, Tennessee, and Texas will disqualify a candidate if his engagement in these activities relate to moonshining or illegal hooch.

In Colonial America, it was customary when taking an oath to place one's right hand on the Volume of Sacred Law, for Christians, this was the Holy Bible. Washington placed his right hand on the Bible and held his hat in his left in 1789. Lincoln, Andrew Johnson, Grant, McKinley, and Hoover all had their right hands on a Bible and their left arms held at their sides. In 1945, Truman supported the Bible in his left hand and rested his right upon it (see photo on page 181). Since 1949, all Presidents have placed their left hands on a Bible and raised their right hands. Queen Elizabeth II placed her right hand on a Bible to take the oath during her coronation in 1953. Where did this practice come from?

Pliny the Elder wrote in *Book 19: The Natural History*, that the ancient Egyptians placed their right hands on a holy onion when swearing an oath of veracity. Freemasons don't use onions because we don't want our secrets to "leek" out. (With the author's apology for the odiferous pun)

"Leg of Mutton Masons" was a derisive term applied to brothers who never attended Lodge functions, with the exception of occasions when free meals were served.

Why is there an officer's chair in the North if there is no officer to sit in the chair? The answer is that the chair was occupied at one time.

Prior to the creation of Deacons, there was a Senior Entered Apprentice and a Junior Entered Apprentice. Two Wardens were seated in the West, the Senior Entered Apprentice in the South and the Junior Entered Apprentice in the North.

Current Masonic ritual states the North is a place of darkness because the Sun never shines through northern windows. But this is only true for those Lodges in England or North of the tropics.

Lee Lodge #209 of Wynesboro, Virginia, faced a crisis in November 1922. The Lodge brethren were divided on an issue that threatened to erupt into a minor Civil War, should the cuspidors remain in the Lodge Room or should all tobacco use be banned during the meetings? By the narrowest of margins, abstention won the day, and a resolution was passed prohibiting the use of tobacco. The cuspidors were removed.

The tobacco free zone prevailed for less than two years before the vicious habit was permitted, but with a limitation. Its indulgence was permitted on the South side of the Lodge Room, but not on the North.

Why only on the South? Because in the original King Solomon's Temple, "no light shown in the North" due to its latitude, and the brethren of Lee Lodge figured the striking of matches would have brought light to the North.

What is the difference between a Masonic obligation and the oath?

The obligation is where a Candidate promises to perform certain actions and refrain from engaging in certain behavior.

The oath is "So help me God."

The Masonic phrase, "To that undiscovered country from whose bourne no traveler returns." was borrowed from playwright William Shakespeare's Hamlet, Act 3, Scene 1, Soliloquy. "But that the dread of something after death, the undiscovere'd country, from whose *bourn*. No traveller returns".

Comprehending the meaning of both phrases requires knowledge that the obsolete early English word *bourn* means boundary.

In United States Masonic Lodges, the oath may not be substituted with an affirmation when taking the Masonic obligation.

This is not the case in English Lodges where Quakers have been conferred as brothers by taking their obligation by affirmation.

Freemasons in Germany were divided into two types when it came to visiting other Lodges, Salute Masons and Letter Masons. Salute Masons proved they were Masons by an examination consisting of a display of signs, grips, passwords, and their knowledge of ritual. Letter Masons or Letter Bearer Masons would gain admission to visit another Lodge by presenting a certificate, under seal, as to their qualifications.

Masons have a Grand Hailing Sign that is used in times of distress or peril to summons aid from brother Masons. Most Masons believe the sign they learned in their Lodge is universally understood by Master Masons everywhere, but this is not the case.

The typical Grand Hailing Sign taught in the United States is not the same as the sign taught in European and English Lodges. In the 1700s, the English sign was called a "Master's Clap".

The American sign is called the "Grand Hail" because one brother is hailing another brother for help.

At the close of the 1700s, Friedrich Ludwig Schroeder had significant impacts on German Masonry. He failed in attempts to move the instruction of the Grand Hailing Sign into the Entered Apprentice Degree ritual. He did succeed in limiting Craft degrees to the present day three, instead of the four degrees or seven degrees or even ten degrees that were in use, depending on which of Germany's several Grand Lodges had chartered the local hall.

On April 12, 2003, at Rosehill Gardens Racetrack in Australia, near Sydney in New South Wales, a racehorse name "Freemason" ran in the premiere BMW Stakes, over a 2400 meter course for three year old horses. Freemason's two minute and 26.8 second time on the clockwise track broke a ten year old record in this Queensland Derby.

It wasn't until 1760 that Masonic Halls, Temples, and Lodges began to receive names befitting of Freemason significance. Prior to 1760, a Lodge was generally known by the name of the tavern or pub in which the members held their meetings.

The fact that early Masons held their meetings in pubs may have had an impact on the manner in which new brother Masons were tested before being advanced to the next degree.

In modern America Masonry, a candidate must recite a formally memorized catechism or examination in the preceding degree before he is Passed or Raised to the next degree. This practice did not exist until 1850, when it was introduced in Louisiana.

Prior to this ritualized proficiency on the lectures, Lodge officers would ask the candidate casual questions over a pint of brew until satisfied that he had an understanding of the preceding degree. If the evening was still young, they would proceed to confer the next degree.

The first record of Freemasons marching in a parade wearing aprons, white gloves, and regalia was in 1738. Until the Great Depression of the 1930s, brothers would gather at the Lodge, don their regalia, and march in procession to a local church for a "Masonic Sermon". The annual event was traditionally held on one of the Saints John Days, Christmas, or Easter.

The first such recorded Masonic Sermon was by Rev. Charles Brockwell in Boston's Christ's Church on December 27, 1749.

The Senior and Junior Wardens have miniature pillars on their pedestals, representing Jachin and Boaz (I Kings 7:21) respectively. These emblems did not exist in 1723 Masonry. They first appeared circa 1760 in London Masonry. At that time, the Wardens carried them into the Lodge in the same manner as the Marshal carried his baton, under their left arms. None of the dozen exposés of Masonic ritual prior to *Three Distinct Knocks,* in 1760, mention the columns.

The April 5, 1759, bylaws of Tandragee Lodge #79 in The Village Tandragee, County Armagh, Ireland (now Northern Ireland), stated, "That there is to be silence at the first clap of the Master's hammer, and likeways at the first stroke of each trenchen struck by the Sen'r and Jun'r Wardens." A Lodge in Chester, England, catalogued within its 1761 inventory, "Two truncheons for the Wardens". Some Irish and English Lodges still refer to these columns as truncheons.

Off the shores of St. Bernard County, Louisiana, is a string of islands named the Chandeleur Chain. This archipelago composes the southernmost tip of Louisiana, even though it is only thirty miles south of Biloxi, Mississippi.

Up until the hurricanes of 1912 shrank the loose subaerial islands, the islands were farmed and had fish processing plants, docks, and wharfs. The islands are part of the Breton National Wildlife Refuge and a critical migrating site for numerous species of birds and nesting spots for Louisiana herons and red egrets.

The lighthouses on the islands have served since the Civil War on an unsteady basis because hurricanes kept sweeping them into the sea. Hurricane Camille in 1969 was particularly devastating. The islands only received media coverage because of the lighthouse; so little was said when Ivan in 2004, followed by Dennis and Katrina in 2005, noticeably reduced the size of the islands. What did capture the public's attention was the Deep Water Horizon Oil Spill of 2010, and that caused a brief flurry of activity among Freemason Internet Conspiracy Theorists.

The southernmost land mass in the chain is Freemason Island, a popular site for recreational fishermen. In May of 2010, Freemason Island was the first landfall of the spreading oil slick. The first images of the deleterious impact of oil on wildlife came from the shores of Freemason Island.

Conspiracy theorists pointed to the name of Freemason Island and began quoting the prophets Haggai and Joel. Their argument being that it was the actions of men which caused the oil to be wasted. This resulted in less available fuel and raised prices. They claimed it was the Freemasons who commanded the spill in order to raise prices and profits worldwide. Theorists pointed both to these scriptures and to the fact that the Wages of a Fellowcraft Mason are: Corn, Wine, and Oil.

"The field is wasted, the land mourneth; for the corn is wasted: the new wine is dried up, the oil languisheth." Joel 1:10

"And I called for a drought upon the land, and upon the mountains, and upon the corn, and upon the new wine, and upon the oil, and upon that which the ground bringeth forth, and upon men, and upon cattle, and upon all the labour of the hands." Haggai 1:11

Masonic Island is a seven acre site on Lake Metigoshe in the Turtle Mountains of North Dakota. It was originally named Park Island. In 1904, the island was owned by Bro. V.J. Noble, who was a member of Tuscan Lodge #44 of North Dakota.

With a dispensation from the Grand Lodge of North Dakota, and the permission of Bro. Noble, the island was cleared in 1906 for the purpose of holding outdoor Masonic conferrals of degrees. Tuscan Lodge was joined by Westhope Lodge #74 for conferrals of three Master Mason Degrees that year. The events were such a success that rituals were held annually for six consecutive years.

When Bro. Noble died, Masons became interested in reviving the conferral of rituals on the island. On November 28, 1933, the Probate Court authorized the sale of the island with a deed to the North Dakota Masonic Foundation for the sum of $277.25.

At the landing dock is a flight of winding concrete stairs consisting of three, five, and seven steps that rise to the representation of a Lodge Room. The significance of the steps might be explained to you if you have a Masonic guide. An altar and officers' chairs were constructed of "beach stones" and mortared cement. Other amenities were added over the years to accommodate the island's use by Royal Arch Masons, Eastern Star, and other attendant Masonic bodies.

Have you ever heard of a "Two and a Half degree Mason"? Enter Bro. David A. Smalley of Chicago, Illinois.

For the non-Mason reader's benefit, Masons present Degrees in sections. Grand Lodges require that all sections of a Degree be conferred during the same meeting.

Standard Lodge #873 had gone from labor to refreshment (taking a break between sections) during the conferral of the Sublime Degree of Master Mason on Bro. Smalley, when the Chicago Fire Marshal interrupted the proceedings and closed the Hall. The date was December 30, 1903, and a fire in the *"absolutely fireproof"* Iroquois Theatre shocked the country with the horrible loss of over six hundred lives. Stringent emergency fire regulations immediately closed all theaters, churches, and buildings housing public gatherings. The Fire Marshall did not permit the Masons to re-enter their building for a fortnight.

When the safety inspections were completed, fire officials granted permission to re-enter the buildings. The Lodge reconvened and completed the degree. In the interim, Bro. Smalley was a labeled a "Two and a Half Degree Mason".

There is no "National Grand Lodge of the United States of America", but there was a Grand Master of and for America.

Colonel Joseph Montfort was born in England in 1724. He was a member of Royal White Hart Lodge #2 in Halifax, North Carolina.

The Fifth Duke of Beaufort, Henry Somersest, was also the Grand Master of the Grand Lodge of Free and Accepted Masons of England. He commissioned Bro. Montfort "The Provincial Grand Master of and for America". In this capacity, Montfort Chartered numerous new Lodges in the colonies.

When North Carolina enacted the Mecklenburg Declaration of Independence on May 20, 1775, Montfort joined the colonial cause.

He died less than two months before the adoption of the Declaration of Independence by the Continental Congress on the Fourth of July in 1776, a year after the Mecklenburg Declaration. Bro. Montfort is buried in the only grave allowed within the grounds of Royal White Hart Lodge.

The USS *Maine* was the nation's second battleship. An explosion on February 15, 1890, sank the vessel in Havana Harbor and precipitated the Spanish-American War. By the end of the war, the United States had acquired the additional territories and lands of Cuba, Guam, Philippine Islands, and Puerto Rico.

In 1911, a giant cofferdam was built around the hull of the *Maine*. In 1912, she was refloated, towed to sea, and scuttled. Many of the men working on her took items as mementos and souvenirs.

Treadwell Lodge #213 in White Post, Virginia, has within its archives a "Good Luck Horseshoe" fashioned from brass reclaimed from the *Maine*. The horseshoe is adorned with the emblems of York Rite Masonry.

A Grand Lodge Degree Team led by Grand Master Norman Byrne opened Chukuni Lodge #660 of Red Lake, Ontario, on June 9, 1990, for the purpose of conferring the First Degree of Masonry on candidate Larry Herbert. Larry was a logger by trade, but on that auspicious day, he became a Mason.

Following the ceremony, the new brother took his bulldozer to the Lodge and reduced it to rubble.

The original Chukuni Lodge #660, as Constituted and constructed in 1948, was drafty to the point that a strong wind could blow out altar candles.

The newly obligated brother and his bulldozer were summoned to "level" the ground upon which the brethren of Chukuni would soon erect their new Masonic edifice.

Years later, as Worshipful Master of the Lodge, Herbert would recount the event with amusement.

The Right Worshipful Lord Mayor of Canterbury
The Right Worshipful Senior Grand Warden
Ye Worshipful Judge Timothy Pierce
The Most Worshipful Judge Peterson
The Most Worshipful Grand Master of California
Worshipful Master George Washington
Worshipful Captain Obadiah Faithful
Worshipful Justice of the Peace Blackburn
Worshipful Company of Chartered Accountants

All of these actual titles use the old definition of "Worshipful" where it means Respected or Honorable and has nothing to do with religion. The Mayor of Canterbury is not Lord Mayor in a Biblical sense and may not even be a secular Lord of English peerage.

The Worshipful Company of Chartered Accountants isn't even a person. It is one of four dozen livery or trade guilds in London.

When Wycliffe published the Bible in 1382, it was written in Middle English. Thus, the fifth commandment reads, "Worchyp thy fadir and thy modir." or "Worship your father and your mother." Modern translations have changed "worship" to "honor".

The title of Worshipful is a sign of respect to the position as well as the person. If the Junior Warden is sitting in the East, he is addressed as "Worshipful Master" even if the Master of the Lodge is in the room. This is the same as calling the commanding officer of a ship "Captain", even if he is of lesser rank.

How important is a chair? For many years Bro. Joseph Denny of Winchester Hiram Lodge #24 of Winchester, Virginia, had a special chair in his possession. His widow donated the chair to the Lodge where it was placed on display. The chair had been used for many years whenever a candidate sat to hear lectures. What gave this chair noteworthy importance is the fact that it was used by a particular candidate, who sat there to listen to the Master's lecture on the Third Degree of Masonry in 1865. The candidate in the chair was none other than future President William McKinley.

When entering cities across America, it is common to see signs bearing the logos or emblems of fraternities and civic groups within that community. In the City of Apopka in Florida, the Masonic symbol of Square and Compass is actually part of the city's official logo.

When Apopka was incorporated in 1882, the city fathers needed a datum or center-point from which to measure out the city limits and layout streets. For their center-point, they choose Orange Masonic Lodge #36, on what became Main Street. The city's metes and bounds were laid out as a measured mile along the four cardinal directions from the Lodge. The Lodge was organized in 1857, and still stands as the oldest original Lodge in the "Sunshine State".

Masonic brethren were instrumental in the agricultural activities of the area. By 1912, the city had earned the nickname of "The Fern City". Railway shipping allowed businesses to expand their product lines by introducing more tropical species. Today, Apopka is known as "The Indoor Foliage Capital of the World".

A Masonic ring is not an official article of Freemason jewelry. A minority of Masons wear their rings with the open points of the compass toward the wrist, "to remind themselves that they are a Masons". Most Masons wear their rings with the tip toward the wrist to inform others that they are Masons.

A Past Master explained why he wore his ring facing outward, "No Mason would wear his Masonic Lapel Pin upside-down to remind himself that he was a Mason, it's to signify to others that he is a Mason."

We all know that Grand Lodges have numerous officers; Grand Standard Bearer, Grand Prelate, Grand Organist, Grand Lecturer, and so forth.

But the Grand Lodge of California has the distinction of having once had "The Most Worshipful Grand Master of the Clam Bake Lodge", George Tisdale Bromley.

Bromley was a Past Master of Union Lodge #58 of Sausalito, as well as, an officer in Royal Arch Chapter #5, and Knights Templar Commandery #1.

Bromley could have entered history textbooks as the First Conductor for the pioneer Sacramento Valley Railroad. When Bromley affiliated with SVR on Feb 22, 1856, it was the first railroad on the Pacific Coast.

Bromley could have entered history textbooks as the developer and operator of the elegant and renowned Pacific Ocean House Hotel constructed in 1866, in the seaside resort town of Santa Cruz, California.

He could have entered history texts as the United States Consul General in Tien Tsin, China, in 1880.

Besides these titles, he and his wife, Sarah Ray, were known as an "all around genial couple and noted hosts".

In his autobiography, W. Bro. Bromley describes but one of his many clam bakes. He could have picked from several he hosted for gubernatorial candidates, for foreign dignitaries, and for visiting federal officials, but he choose to describe the one held October 11, 1877, for the Grand Lodge officers. In Bromley's own words, here is an account of that famous clam bake:

"The beach at Sausalito was the place appointed for the bake. The forty bags of seaweed were gathered from the shores of the bay, and the cobblestones were taken from the city. As none but members of the Grand Lodge were expected to be present except those who assisted in preparing the bake, I had any number of volunteers, so that my labor consisted in seeing that others did the work. At twelve o'clock on Wednesday of the Grand Lodge week, the Lodge adjourned and all marched in a body to the wharf, where a spacious steamer, chartered for the occasion, was in waiting to receive them.

"Upon arriving at the beach, those six hundred Past Master Masons were arranged on the slope, where they witnessed the modus operandi of building up a clambake.

"When all was in readiness the fires were raked from the cobbles and they were covered with seaweed to a depth of a foot and a half. Then, over the seaweed was spread a sheet of muslin, in the center of which was dumped eighteen bushels of soft-shelled clams. There were also the following: Large quantities of several varieties of fish delicately cleaned and seasoned, wrapped in white paper, lamb and pork chops, chicken, sausage, green corn, the husks having been stripped down, butter and salt applied, and the husks replaced and the ends fastened. A large quantity of sweet and common potatoes rounded out the wonderful collection, and it was then covered with another sheet of muslin on top of which were piled several feet of seaweed, and over all were placed the empty sea weed sacks, and thus ended the building up of the clam bake.

"When time was up, and all had assembled to witness the unveiling of the clambake, and when Grand Master Brown had called everybody to order, there was brought within the circle a table upon which was a lovely casket.

"When the table was put in place, Past Grand Master Charles L. Wiggin, in his own eloquent way of doing those things, presented me with the casket, which contained a splendid set of table cutlery."

Truly, the genial W. Bro. Bromley was indeed "The Most Worshipful Grand Master of the Clam Bake Lodge".

An account of an 1832 Masonic funeral at Inverness Shire, Scotland, relates that, "As were the custom, a bowl turned of acacia were placed on the brother's well chest and each passing brother did place a pinch of salt upon."

The wood of the acacia was called *shittim* by the ancient Hebrews, who planted it at the head of graves as a funerary symbol signifying the immortality of the soul. Exodus 25:10 & 25:23 relates God commanding Moses to build the Ark for the tabernacle out of acacia wood. In Freemasonry, the acacia also represents the immortality of the soul and a sprig is often placed with the body of a deceased brother.

In the Gospel of Mark, salt represents friendship. This is the same meaning attributed to salt by the third century Diocletian martyr and exegetical Biblical author, Saint Pierius, more commonly known as Origen the Younger.

Helvetian Masons still use salt as part of their symbolism. It is a practice in Switzerland among Freemasons to present a gift of salt when welcoming new neighbors.

Scrimshaw is the old art of engraving designs on whale teeth, shells, antlers, bone, or ivory and highlighting the channels with tar or lampblack. The pictured giant ostrich egg depicting Washington dates from 1852. Masonic scrimshaw was popular in the mid-1800s for cane tops and razor handles. Most scrimshaw on the market today is plastic "shamshaw".

Hollenbeck Masonic Lodge #319 of Los Angeles, California, was Chartered on October 11, 1894. By all accounts, it was blessed both by a large charter membership and by an excellent first Worshipful Master in Trowbridge H. Ward. Ward's personable manner helped Hollenbeck to grow by more than a dozen new members each year for many years.

One of Hollenbeck's famous "new members" was Jimmy Doolittle, later to be famous for the "Doolittle Raid on Tokyo" in World War Two. Doolittle's petition for membership in Hollenbeck was during World War One. Before degrees could be conferred, Doolittle, received orders to deploy overseas from Louisiana.

Both California and Louisiana Grand Lodges granted a dispensation for Doolittle to be made a "California Mason" in Louisiana, at Lake Charles Lodge #16. When the day came, Lake Charles was storm damaged, and an emergency dispensation was issued to conduct all the rituals in one day at Elk Temple. Doolittle later continued his Masonic journey through Scottish Rite and Shrine.

If Bro. Doolittle had received his degrees in storm damaged Lake Charles, he might not have noticed any difference from Hollenbeck.

Because of leaky roof problems in the early lodge, one of the *special duties* of the Senior Warden, when conducting candidates around the Lodge Room during degree rituals, was to hold an umbrella above the candidate when it was raining.

The brothers of Hollenbeck may have needed a mop and pail after rain storms, but they weren't the first Freemasons to make use of those tools.

Nights when degrees were to be conferred on candidates during the 1700s were referred to as "mop and pail" evenings. This name was derived from a practice that was peculiar to the nature of the early meeting places. Because the meetings were in temporary quarters such as pubs, designs necessary to the ritual were drawn on the floor with chalk or charcoal. At the close of the evening, the designs were washed away with a mop and pail.

Some unnamed brother, who tired of mopping and hauling pails of water to and from the lodge, painted the designs on a sheet of canvas that could be rolled or folded and stored until needed again. These permanent canvas cloths came to be known as "Lodge Carpets".

CHAPTER 5

OOPS, STUFF THAT'S WRONG

The producers of the immensely popular and entertaining television show *Mythbusters* aired an episode during their third season entitled, *Shop Til You Drop Special*. The April 6, 2005, episode featured some of the suppliers the show's stars have used to acquire unusual items needed to explore the myths and urban legends put to scrutiny during their shows. As a highlight segment, co-star Adam Savage took the viewers on a tour of his house.

Mr. Savage displayed what he called his "weirdest object", an item he had acquired at a flea market. The oddity was a pair of copper, steel, glass, and leather goggles with flip-up metallic caps covering red glass lenses in the eyepieces.

Mr. Savage called the antique object exhibited in his hands, "Masonic Initiation Goggles".

Since time immemorial, candidates receiving degrees in Freemasonry are "hoodwinked" with a cloth blindfold covering their eyes during a portion of their initiation. They are never blindfolded with goggles made of metals or minerals. In

Masonic ritual, there is no need for rapidly concealing and exposing the candidate's vision with red lenses.

Three internet auction sites have listed this style of goggle as being used by the Independent Order of Odd Fellows during their initiation ceremony where alleged repeated exposure and concealment of the candidates vision is required, hence the flip-up caps.

These are not Masonic goggles. Apparently, the Mythbuster's Masonic myth is busted.

Every Mason has read a Trestleboard snippet saying that Freemasons disguised as Indians boarded English merchant vessels in Boston harbor on December 16, 1773, and threw bales of tea into the briny water. Problem #1, Samuel Adams, who led the event, was not a Freemason and there is no documented proof of any specific Freemason involvement.

Fear not that our Masonic brothers sat around drinking latte grandees as their only rebellion against the Stamp Act. Boston Harbor of 1773 was not the site of the first raid on a British vessel.

King George III had dispatched Lt. William Dudingston as commander of the armed schooner, HMS *Gaspee,* with orders to put an end to colonial smuggling.

On June 9, 1772, Dudingston was in aggressive pursuit of the packet sloop *Hannah* under the command of Thomas Lindsey. Captain Lindsey's only hope of out-running the British warship and the hail of cannonballs splashing around him was a risky pass over the edges of the Namquid Point shallows. The *Hannah* safely passed the shallows. But, the aggressive Lt. Dudingston ran the deeper draft *Gaspee* aground, during an ebbing tide.

Lindsey sailed on into Providence and eventual word reached Masonic Grand Master, Abraham Whipple, of St. John's Lodge #1 that the *Gaspee* would not be afloat until high tide at three the next morning.

That evening, Freemasons gathered in Sabin Tavern for their usual meeting. The men replaced the practice of Masonic ritual with melting lead for bullet molds, as they were in short supply of shot for their muskets. The Lodge minutes for the evening reflect, "No meeting tonight, more pressing business at hand."

Under Whipple's command, eight long boats with muffled oars departed from Ferrer's Wharf and approached the *Gaspee* under cover of darkness. Dudingston was shot during the boarding, but survived. His crew was captured, and his ship set ablaze. The *Gaspee* burned to her waterline before the fire reached her powder magazines. The resulting explosion finished off what remained of her hull.

Whipple went on to become the first Commodore of the Rhode Island Navy, a precursor to the Continental Navy, and was an instrumental Captain during the Revolutionary War, until taken as a prisoner-of-war in 1780.

The chiseled tribute on his tombstone reads, "Sacred to the memory of Commodore Abraham Whipple whose name, skill and courage, will ever remain the pride and boast of his country. In the late Revolution he was the first in the seas to hurl defiance at proud Britain; gallantly leading the way to arrest from the mistress of the ocean, her scepter, and there to wave the star-spangled banner. He also conducted to sea, the first square-rigged vessel, ever built on the Ohio, opening to commerce resources beyond calculation."

First Masonic Myth About
Rear-Admiral Byrd at the Poles

Since October 1935, Lodge trestleboards have reported that Rear-Admiral Richard Evelyn Byrd and Col. Bernt Balchen tossed a Masonic Flag out of their plane as they flew over the North Pole. Oops, it didn't happen.

Col. Bernt Balchen, USAF, was responsible for bringing attention to doctored flight logs and false sextant sightings that discredited Lt. Cmdr. Byrd's claim to have flown over the North Pole with pilot Floyd Bennett in May 1926.

With this history between the two men, it seems peculiar that Byrd selected Balchen as the pilot for his attempt at the South Pole three years later.

Why did Byrd select Balchen? There were two reasons. First, the Norseman was the best cold weather pilot in the world. Second, Byrd's financial backers wanted Balchen involved because the pilot's reputation was impeccable.

On November 19, 1929, with Bernt Balchen at the controls of a Ford Tri-motor named the *"Floyd Bennett"* after Byrd's pilot on the North Pole adventure, the South Pole was reached by air.

Byrd had been a member of Federal Lodge #1 of the District of Columbia since March 19, 1921, and had affiliated with Kane Lodge #454 of New York on September 18, 1929.

Balchen was a member of Norseman Lodge #878 of Brooklyn, New York, and of Kismet Temple Shrine.

As Byrd and Balchen flew over the South Pole, each man tossed a Masonic flag from the plane. Balchen also tossed his red bejeweled fez from Kismet Temple Shrine.

Col. Balchen went on to fly the first balloon flight carrying US Mail across the Atlantic. The mail included envelopes bearing Masonic Cachets for philatelists.

While preparing for her successful solo transatlantic flight of May 1932, Amelia Earhart hired Balchen to modify her Lockheed Vega for the crossing.

Balchen flew 166 covert missions behind enemy lines for the OSS (it later became the CIA) during World War Two. During his career, this Mason received military and aviation awards that are too numerous to list in this chapter.

Second Byrd at the Poles Myth

Byrd was back in Little America, Antarctica, in 1933-1935. Sixty of the eighty-two men in the expedition were Freemasons. This adventure spawned the second often reported myth that Byrd formed the first Lodge in Antarctic under a New Zealand Constitution.

The *Pacific Lodge Broadcast* of August 1935 printed a facsimile of a Tyler's Registry that bore the handwritten legend, "Attendance Book, 1st Antarctica Lodge – No. 777 – N.Z.C. Little America, February 5th – 1935". The echoes of this false note have reverberated throughout Masonic Halls for over seventy-five years.

Thanks to letters from men actually involved in the 1935 meeting and research published in the *New Zealand Freemason* in 1982 and 1983, we have a complete account of the Antarctic event.

On January 27, 1935, The SS *Jacob Ruppert* arrived in Antarctica to replenish supplies and to remove old equipment, as well as, exchanging a number of the men. The cargo ship was named for one of the expedition's financial backers, Jacob Ruppert. Former Congressman Ruppert owned the New York Yankees during the Babe Ruth years, and his brewery produced New York's number one beer, Knickerbocker.

The *Ruppert* was loaded and ready to depart from the Bay of Whales on February 5, 1935. On her deck was the Ford Tri-motor of South Pole fame, headed for the Ford Museum in Dearborn, Michigan.

While still at sea, Freemasons in the *Ruppert's* crew had proposed holding a meeting in the mess hall when the ship arrived on station in Antarctica. Informal plans were prepared and supplies gathered.

The crew selected an imaginary name for the Lodge, "First Antarctic Lodge No. 777, New Zealand Constitution". New Zealand was selected because it had the closest Grand Lodge to Little America and many of the scientists were from New Zealand.

Dr. Ross Hepburn of Christchurch wrote of the meeting, "Bro. Byrd and others on the ice were invited to be present and attended. The lodge was opened on the First Degree and Bro. Mitchell gave a lecture on the First Tracing Board. The lodge was then closed, never to meet again, and most of the evening was spent in the refectory where experiences and reminiscences were exchanged." Besides Bro. Mitchell as Master pro-tem, Bro. Sissons acted as the senior warden pro-tem.

W.Bro. J.G. Sissons of Mokoia Lodge #213 of Wellington, New Zealand, was a principal organizer. He was on a leave of absence from the New Zealand Post Office and was the Rupert's radio officer. He wrote of the event, "The meeting was purely an informal shipboard one and nothing more. There was no charter from any Grand Lodge and Bro. Mitchell, the acting master, was not in fact installed master. The number 777 was merely the invention of the brethren concerned. To give the meeting some semblance of Masonic flavor they gave the proposed Lodge a number and appointed officers for the sole purpose of opening and closing the Lodge. The officers were limited to members of the ship's crew as rehearsals had to be held beforehand, but Bro. Byrd and others on the ice were invited to be present and attended the meeting."

As to how the meeting gained such a level of notoriety, there was a letter written by W.Bro. Jim Sissons forty-seven years after the event that explained, "... Bro. Mitchell returned to America and lectured at many lodges allegedly stating that the meeting was held under the New Zealand Constitution. This could not be forgiven as it was not true. ... It was Bro. Mitchell's statement that caused all the trouble, otherwise the episode would have been forgotten as such meetings usually are. Bro. Mitchell was evidently so intent on publicity that he pushed himself into the limelight at every opportunity. Other lodges would accept his word and arranged publicity accordingly. ... I am 86 now and I hope that, in the short time that will probably be remaining for me, I will not hear any more about this troublesome subject."

Whether an officially sanctioned meeting or not, there was no need for the Tiler to check for women eavesdroppers as it was two weeks later on February twentieth that Caroline Mikkelsen, the wife of the Captain of the Norwegian whaler *Thorshaven*, set foot on the continent as the first woman in Antarctica.

Fear that the encroaching ice would buckle her plates after unloading her cargo of 400 tons of supplies, 16,000 gallons of gasoline, and 12,500 gallons of crude oil for heating, the crew of SS *Jacob Ruppert* departed in the afternoon, unaware of the notoriety and controversy that awaited them on their return to a warmer clime.

Technically, the meeting aboard the SS *Jacob Ruppert* was a shipboard meeting and not "on" the continent of Antarctica. Seven Masons in the United States Navy put an end to that issue on February 6, 1947.

In the midst of an Antarctic snowstorm, three commissioned officers and four petty officers met in a paraffin coated duck-canvas tent for the purpose of Masonic communication. Brother William Blades took photographs and Lieutenant Commander McCoy documented the event in a letter to West Roxbury Lodge of Boston, Massachusetts:

The following brothers were present: Wm. R. Blades, CQM, USN, West Roxbury Lodge, Boston, Mass.; R. H. Jones, CCS, USN, North Carolina Maiden Lodge No. 692; Paul Saylor, ACETM, USN, Westville Lodge No. 192, Westville, Indiana; E. F. Fulmer, AMMI, USN, Oleeta Lodge No. 145, Miami Springs, Florida; J. C. McCoy, Lt. Comdr. USN, Albert J. Russell Lodge No. 12G, Jacksonville, Florida; F. G. Dustin, Lt. Comdr. USN, Morrisville Lodge Morrisville, Vermont, and A. D. Wildey, Lt. (J.G.) USN, Naval Lodge No. 4,

Washington, D.C. Lt. Comdr. F. G. Dustin was elected to preside and Wm. R. Blades, CQM, to act as secretary of the momentous occasion. The following statement was offered by the chairman:

"My dear brothers, we are gathered here today at the bottom of the world, a small group of men representing the brothers of our respective Lodges and our brethren all over the universe. We are members of an important function that our government has directed and assigned certain duties. I know you join in this feeling of pride I have as a citizen and as a Mason, that we, through our government are privileged to be standing on this virgin territory.

We Masons gathered here today are standing in a flimsy canvas tent. The canvas beats and strains. It is snowing and a blizzard is in the making. There are hundreds of feet of snow beneath us and around us as far as we can see. The elements in this area run wild and unharnessed. High velocity blizzards race across the unknown and then all is calm, but the rigors of this land have us not in fear. A great leader has placed the required tools in our hands and guides us with his knowledge. We know the result of the blizzard means a few more inches of snow, a mountain peak exposed or covered and the inevitable calm and peace.

Brothers, I close with this message: Let us call the recent war our Antarctic blizzard; our fallen brethren, the covered mountains after the blizzard; the cessation of battle, the inevitable calm that we know we will have here in a few hours. The sight of this peaceful, hardly describable continent should therefore act as a tonic of a type that we might take back to civilization to stimulate and direct unselfish peacemakers into decisions of calmness, peace and plenty for the peoples of the world."

Every US Civics student has read the account of Grand Master George Washington leading the procession of Virginian Masons to the future site of the United States Capital Building and conducting the cornerstone laying ceremony in the northeast corner of the site, as was the Masonic custom. The story is nice, but those facts are wrong.

The ceremony of September 18, 1793, began in Virginia at Alexandria Lodge #22, but the ceremony was conducted under the auspices of the Grand Lodge of Maryland as the site of the Capital was within Maryland's Masonic Jurisdiction. The first leg of the procession to President's Square was led by a marching band, not by President Washington.

Grand Marshall Clotworthy Stephenson then led the second procession to the construction site in a column two abreast. When the column parted, the Grand Sword Bearer lead the way, followed by Grand Master *Pro Tempore* of Maryland Joseph Clark on the left, Brother George Washington in the center, and the Worshipful Master of Alexandria Lodge #22 Elisha C. Dick on the right. Also following the Sword Bearer to the cavazion trench were the City of Washington Commissioners and additional Worshipful Masters from visiting Lodges.

Washington presided, with Clark, R. W. Elisha C. Dick, and Valentine Reintzel, the Master of Lodge #9 of Maryland in the District of Columbia, assisting in laying the cornerstone in the southeast corner of the site, not in the northeast corner.

Grand Master *Pro Tempore* Joseph Clark delivered the keynote address, followed by a volley of canon fire and the barbeque of a five hundred pound ox.

CHAPTER 6

DON'T TINKER WITH THE TILER

In Symbolic Masonry, the Tiler or Tyler is a Master Mason whose duty it is to challenge all those who approach the Lodge Room door and verify that all who enter are Masons who are duly qualified. To be duly qualified, a Mason must have been advanced through the proper degree of work for the meeting, be current with his dues, be clad in the proper apron, and have permission of the Master to enter.

In ancient stonemason guilds, Tilers guarded the door against eavesdroppers and *cowans*. They still serve this function today. The short definition for cowans is that they could be hired to build walls of loose stones without mortar or cement, were not yet apprenticed to a Master Mason, and had no right to attend or vote at secret guild meetings.

In a typical Lodge, the Tiler sits outside the Lodge Room door in a Tiler's room, armed with a symbolic sword resting at his side or mounted on the wall. By tradition, the ceremonial sword had a wavy blade representing a ray from a blazing star. Modern Tilers may bear a ceremonial straight military sword or curved cavalry saber donated by a brother. Others make do with a cross-shaped Christian sword donated by a Knight Templar.

The Tiler has not been armed with a sword through all of Masonic history. In early Freemasonry, the Tiler was "armed with the proper implement of his office", which was appropriately, a trowel used for setting tiles.

The Tiler at Cariboo Lodge #469 in Barkerville, British Columbia, Canada, required neither sword nor trowel to perform his job. Cariboo had a "Silent Tyler" that was designed to keep out "wild men and some equally wild women". Barkerville must have been an interesting town in the 1860s.

When Cariboo was constructed in 1869, the brethren designed and installed an outdoor stairway that was the only avenue of egress into the second story Lodge Room. This stairway was hinged at one end, allowing it to be raised once the brethren were assembled on the upper floor. With the Silent Tyler raised, access into the Lodge was effectively cut off, thus thwarting any eavesdroppers and prying eyes.

This safeguard acted in a manner one might liken to a drawbridge. The stairway on the left side of the building was raised and lowered by means of an operating wheel and pulley system installed in the Tiler's room.

A latecomer could petition for entrance by tugging a cord that ran to an upstairs bell. Due to the security of this arrangement, the Lodge's Tiler served as both the Inner Guard and Tiler. In 1936, Cariboo Lodge and their Silent Tyler were destroyed by fire.

Prior to the advent of computerized e-mails and cellphones, it was the duty of the Tilers to deliver summonses to special meetings requiring urgent business. Tilers were paid for providing this service.

Not all Tilers were adept at keeping the business of the Lodge meetings secret. There was one case where the Tiler himself was discovered to be the dreaded eavesdropper.

The February 23, 1815, minutes of the Lodge of Probity #61 of Halifax, West Yorkshire, England, reveal, "The Transactions of this Lodge having been repeatedly divulged to the other Lodges in this Town, and turned into ridicule; and as every member declares his innocence, it was thought the Tyler must have been the Tale-bearer; in consequence a ballot took place, when he was, by the unanimous consent of the members, discharged, and Bro. Thomas Bradley was then proposed for Tyler, who was unanimously approved of."

Halifax was long noted as a citizenry with harsh law enforcement. A replica of the Halifax Gibbet used to decapitate criminals still stands in the town. The Tale-bearing Tiler is lucky to have merely lost his job and not his head.

Apparently Bro. Bradley was not fully up to the task either, for in the minutes of June 1, 1815, it was recorded, "That in consequence of the inability of our present Tyler to fulfill the arduous duties of the Lodge, it was unanimously agreed that an Inner Guard should be made to assist him, and that he should have half the fees of Initiation, the Tyler the other half; also that he should have 6d (d stood for *denarius*, an old symbol for penny) for liquor allowed each Lodge night. Bro. Bates proposed Dan Sugden for this office, which was agreed to. Brethren who are Inner Guards, or who aspire to be such, should take particular note of this resolution."

In 1846, Bro. Simon Lundry of Charleston Lodge #35 in Charleston, Illinois, was in dire financial straits and could not afford to pay the fees to receive his Fellowcraft and Master Mason Degrees. The December minutes of the Lodge reflect that Brother Lundry possessed something the Lodge needed, and they agreed to accept it in exchange for his fees, a sword for their Tiler.

Even though the Tiler and Organist are officers of a Lodge, they need not be members of the particular Lodges where they perform their duties. In early Masonry, it was a common practice for multiple Lodges to hire the same brother as Tiler of their several Lodges.

In 1903, Hollywood Masonic Lodge #355 (originally of Hollywood, now in Tarzana, California), hired an outside brother from an eastern Lodge as their Tiler. Only after the Tiler's death, when they were preparing the brother's Masonic history for his memorial, did they discovered that the man entrusted to the job of regularly checking for their current dues receipts was himself suspended from his Lodge for non-payment of dues, for a period of some twenty-plus years.

At various times, Tilers have summoned brethren to Lodge meetings by means of bells and even cannon fire. The Tiler of Waco Lodge #92 in Waco, Texas, had a method that was not only unique, but also well suited to the cattle-town of its day. He would blow a cow horn from the Lodge Room window.

When the Grand Orient of France chartered La Loge Française of Richmond, Virginia, in 1849, it became the first French speaking Lodge in the United States. Later that year on November 1, members of the Grand Lodge of Virginia and St. Johns Lodge #36 met with the brothers of La Loge Française in the first recognition of a "regular" or English Lodge and a "clandestine" or French Rite Lodge to take place in America. As a result of the fraternal feelings that permeated the meeting, the Grand Lodge of Virginia communicated with the Grand Orient, and a Charter was granted La Loge Française by Virginia on December 17, 1850.

The ceremony surrounding the investiture of the Charter included the presentation of flags for the

Commonwealth of Virginia, France, and the United States. Both Masonic Craft and York Rite ceremonies were included and translated into both French and English for the guests. In 1890, the name of the Lodge was changed to its present form, Fraternal Lodge #53.

Fraternal is an appropriate name for the Lodge on many levels. One such level is the account of how it came to pass that Masonry in Richmond was saved during the Civil War. An official account of the event was published by Fraternal Lodge in 1874, and involves the heroic actions of La Loge Française's Tiler, Thomas Angel.

According to the records, Bro. Angel acted "with commendable zeal, energy and presence of mind" while the Union Army was bearing down on Richmond. Taking his duty as "guarding the entrance" to the Lodge most seriously, the Tiler gathered together not only the Lodge jewels, documents, and regalia from La Loge Française, but also from the other Lodges within Richmond. After securing the items within La Loge Française, he clothed himself in a lamb skin apron, the "time honored badge of a Mason", and assumed his duties at the door to the Lodge to await the arrival of Yankee troops.

His wait was short. When the Yankees marched on Richmond, a Major Stevens found Bro. Angel at his post. Impressed with the Tiler's zeal, the Major assigned a Masonic brother within his command, Sergeant Gibbs, to remain on post with the Tiler and see that "none passed but such as were duly authorized". The Major also sent men to protect the home of the Tiler's daughter. Gibbs and Angel stood guard for the ensuing three months.

The Tiler of a Lodge must be a Master Mason, even if the Lodge is being opened on an Entered Apprentice Degree or Fellowcraft Degree. It is the Tiler's duty to properly examine approaching Brethren of the Lodge and visiting brothers to determine that they are Masons. As the next story indicates, this rule has not always been followed.

This story begins in the small Indian village of Wyandotte in the Kansas Territory. The Wyandot or Wendat Indians, who were called the Huron by the French in Canada, were well settled in the area when the white man came and began to build cabins. It was not until the treaty of 1855 that the emigration of men and families from the East began. The village didn't become a town of 1,000 until the spring of 1857, with the arrival of the steamboat. The steamboat from St. Louis brought men with money for land and property speculation. That was when Silas Armstrong's eight-room house was converted into a hotel, and its second floor stairway became the town's impromptu gallows. Eventually, Wyandotte grew to become part of Kansas City, Kansas. But our story takes place in 1854, before the boom of '57.

It was August 11, 1854, when the first Masonic communication occurred in what is modern day Kansas. The setting was that rustic Wyandot Indian village. The Grand Lodge of Missouri had granted a dispensation in July to form a Lodge, and the August 11 meeting was called to elect and install officers of Grove Lodge. Two years later, when the Grand Lodge of Kansas was formed, the Lodge received its present name of Wyandotte Lodge #3.

Even though the Governor of the Territory, William Walker, lived in Wyandotte, his home was only a small one-story framed log house, ill-suited for a gathering. His brother, Matthew R. Walker, owned a larger one-story brick house that was further away from the noise of the blacksmith's anvil and Indian Council House, so the meeting was held at Matthew's.

J.M. Chevinton was installed as Master of Grove Lodge by the attending Deputy Grand Master of Missouri, G. Piper. Matthew Walker was the Senior Warden. But, it was the Tiler who received the most attention in Masonic history.

With such a small population, there were an insufficient number of brothers to fill the necessary chairs and to have a Tiler. Mrs. Walker, a Native American Wyandot, was conscripted to act as Tiler. Besides being the first woman Tiler in the history of the Craft, Mrs. Walker went on in Masonry to become the first Grand Matron of the Eastern Star of Kansas. She was also the first Native American to hold either post of Tiler or Grand Matron.

The year 1828 was the height of the anti-Masonic fervor arising out of a controversy called "The Morgan Affair". During this period, local anti-Masonic authorities resorted to unlawfully seizing Lodges and Lodge possessions. Morgan Park Lodge #999 of Chicago, Illinois, found itself in such a pickle when their Lodge was sealed by county officials.

As the years passed, the anti-Masonic fanaticism quelled. Brethren of the Lodge wished to reopen, but lacked their Charter, lights, officer regalia, and tools of the craft. They called a meeting to brainstorm a solution for their dilemma. Much to their astonishment, the Lodge Tiler, Past Master Charles M. Gray, walked into the meeting with all of the above items. Needless to say, the brethren were surprised, but not dumbfounded enough that they failed to ask how the possessions had escaped impoundment.

Gray explained that he had foreseen the possible seizure. As Tiler, he had the keys to the Lodge and storage areas and was able to secure the items in advance of the approaching authorities. Thereupon, he'd entrusted the items to the care of "a maiden friend". Gray went on to state, "She deposited them between the straw and feather ticks of her bed, where they remained unmolested."

CHAPTER 7

CLOTHES MAKE THE MASON

Officers and brethren of Masonic Lodges are noted for their reserved dress. When conferring degrees, officers traditionally wear tuxedos or dark suits. Sideliners at degree conferrals are expected to wear jackets. Not all Masonic Lodges adhere to this dress code.

There have been more than a handful of Lodges where the wearing of bib-overalls has been the accepted, and sometimes deemed the required, fashion of the day. One Lodge in particular stands out in this category. Before we discuss that Lodge, let's address nine others.

The brethren of Prairieville "Poetry" Lodge #253 of Terrell, Texas, traditionally wear white shirts with their bib-overalls on Election Night and announced Stated Meetings.

The men of Bowling Green Lodge #73 of Bowling Green, Kentucky, dressed in bib-overalls when conferring outdoor degrees by kerosene lamplight.

Within the same Grand Lodge, the members of Miles Lodge #341 of West Point, Kentucky, wear "Tux-Bibs". They get the "Tux" part by wearing long sleeve dress shirts and bowties with their overalls.

The early membership of Pleasant Grove Lodge #22 of Pleasant Grove, Minnesota, was composed mostly of farmers who arrived at Lodge meetings from their labors, dressed as they were in the fields. This explains the origin of the Lodge nickname, "The Bib-Overall Lodge".

The brothers of Chetek Lodge #227 of Chetek, Wisconsin, saw no reason to change their dress code in 2009 on "Bib-Overalls Night" just because the Grand Master of Wisconsin, John Wilke, was paying an Official Visit that evening.

Members of Rutland Lodge #298 of Macon, Georgia, reflect the agricultural industry around their Lodge by wearing bib-overalls during the summer months.

After hosting their annual Valentine's Day social and dinner, the wives and widows retire for an invigorating post-prandial dice game of Bunko, while the men of Union Lodge #593 of Union, Missouri, cordially open the Lodge wearing their Black-ties, white shirts, and bib-overalls.

Retired railway employees of King George Lodge #59 of Calgary, Alberta, Canada, have a special Degree Team. The men confer degrees wearing striped Engineer's bib-overalls. Unlike the fun "Railroad Degree" performed in York Rite Chapters, the men of King George confer a formal Fellowcraft Degree annually in October. Another concession to their railroad history is the Master's gavel. He doesn't rap a wooden gavel. The Master rings a brass bell from a locomotive engine.

Skykomish, Washington, is a town with a long railroading history and the home to Skykomish Masonic Lodge #259. In 2011, they even wore their striped Engineer's bib-overalls during the Official Visit of the District Deputy.

It's now time to mention the most famous bib-overall wearing Lodge in the country, Farmers Lodge #168 of Kinross, Iowa. What makes this Lodge the most famous? It isn't the fact that they proudly bill themselves as *The Only Lodge in Iowa With a Dress Code of Bib Overalls*. It isn't that visiting Masons are asked to wear bib-overalls whenever possible. It isn't because they have been written up in trestleboard newsletters across the country. It is because Farmers Lodge and their dress code were featured in the August 2009 issue of

Freemasonry Tasmania, the monthly *Journal of the Antient, Free and Accepted Masons of Tasmania*. And we all know that Tasmania is a devil of a place to get recognized.

This author recognizes that some Masons may consider Tux-Bib Overalls a bit too formal, well, fear not, for many another Lodge has opted on occasion for colorful Hawaiian shirts for Stated Meetings and conferrals of Degrees. We'll skip "Fun Dinner Nights", Luaus, and "Karaoke Night", while we list a few Stated Meetings.

Huntington Beach Lodge #380 of Huntington Beach, California.
Hollywood Lodge #355 of Tarzana, California.
Atascadero Lodge #493 of Atascadero, California.
S.W. Hackett Masonic Lodge #574 of San Diego, California.
Southern California Masonic Lodge #529 in Playa del Rey.
King David's Lodge #209 of San Luis Obispo, California.

Okay, there seems to be a trend developing, but there are Lodges in states other than California who like shirts depicting gaudy flowers, woody station wagons, hula girls, surf boards, and assorted beer coasters.

Forest Lodge #130 of Wausau, Wisconsin, for a posting examination on the Master Mason Degree.
Dunedin Lodge #192 of Dunedin, Florida, for the Initiation of an Entered Apprentice.
Fidalgo Lodge #77 of Anacortes, Washington, with awards for the best Hawaiian shirt at the Stated Meeting.
Ridgefield Daylight Lodge #237 of Vancouver, Washington, to confer double Second Degrees.

Henrico Union Lodge #130 of Petersburg, Virginia, for a
Table Lodge Joint Communication with local
Lodges.

And Stated Meetings at: Orient Lodge #395 of
Wilmington, North Carolina; Mt. Carmel Lodge
#133 of Warrenton, Virginia; Grants Pass Masonic
Lodge #84 of Grants Pass, Oregon; Boise Masonic
Lodge #2 of Boise, Idaho; Cuyahoga Falls Lodge
#735 of Cuyahoga Falls, Ohio; Winter Park Lodge
#239 of Winter Park, Florida.

Sutherland Lodge #174 of Sutherland, Florida, held a
"Hobo Festival" in 1915 to raise money for the construction of
the Morton F. Plant Hospital. When the twenty-bed hospital
opened the next year, it was the first hospital in nearby
Clearwater. By 2011, the hospital had grown to 687 beds.

The highlight of the 1915 charity event was a parade of
Masons dressed in hobo costumes. The next year, neighboring
Dunedin Lodge #192 was Chartered. To raise money for
mortgage payments, Dunedin hosted their own "Hobo
Parties".

Sutherland continued holding their Hobo event through
the years of World War Two. Dunedin held their parties
through the 1930s and started them again in the 1950s.
Activities continued to include the spirited - but never rowdy –
Hobo Parade, the presentation of a Hobo Degree Ritual, and
contests for Best Dressed Hobo (isn't that an oxymoron?) and
Best Teller of Hobo Tales. Their March 22, 1951, event
featured fish, grits, and pickles; probably no worse than the
deep-fat fried Twinkies at modern county fairs. Fortunately,
the menu changed to "Mulligan Stew" in the 1960s.

The Official Dress Code of the Victorian Masonic
Motorcycle Association for brothers when visiting Lodges

states, "Minimum of clean black denim jeans or *leather trousers*, black boots or shoes, white long sleeve shirt and bow tie, *black leather vest* along with the appropriate Masonic regalia."

The brethren of Paul Revere Lodge in Brockton, Massachusetts, have a Colonial Degree Team that dresses in period outfits.

St. John's Lodge #1 in Portsmouth, New Hampshire, has conferred Degrees with officers clad in a manner of colonial dress befitting the station of their office.

Hastings Lodge #50 in Hasting Nebraska, has an annual George Washington Birthday Degree where the officers are garbed in colonial attire and powdered wigs (actually, white wigs without the powder).

Kilts are common in Scottish Lodges, but not unheard of in American Lodges. The Detroit Masonic News reported in 1921 that the district's Highland Degree Team conferred First and Third Degrees while visiting Temple Lodge. The team was composed of kilt-clad brothers from three local Lodges (Detroit Lodge #2, Zion Lodge #1, and Union Lodge #3) and one Scottish Lodge (Kilwinning). Instead of accompanying organ music, the team supplied bagpipers.

No ritual is as solemn as a Masonic funeral service, which makes the 2011 printed announcement of Bro. Don Wailes' memorial service of Eastgate Masonic Lodge #630 of Des Moines, Iowa, noteworthy; "Casual dress is requested and Hawaiian shirts preferred".

CHAPTER 8

THE CIRCUS COMES TO MASONRY

There are twenty-two Shriners Hospitals for Children spanning North America. These not-for-profit hospitals have provided free orthopedic, burn, and spinal injury treatment to numberless children for eighty years without regard to religion, race, or financial ability. Known as "The World's Greatest Philanthropy", the members of the Ancient Arabic Order of the Nobles of the Mystic Shrine are often referred to as the partying or clowning side of Masonry. Whenever there is a festive parade, Shrine clowns on mini-motorcycles or in garish clown-cars can be found bringing smiles to young and old alike.

The Shrine clowns regularly visit local hospitals, bringing joy and moments of frivolity to an otherwise sterile hospital setting and curing *coulrophobia* (fear of clowns).

The annual Shrine Circus travels the country from Spring through Fall raising monies to support Shriners Children's Hospitals. Many world-famous clowns and circus entertainers have performed with the Shrine Circus. What few people realize is the historic connection between "circus folk" and Freemasonry. This chapter highlights Masonic entertainers associated with "The Big Tent".

When discussing the circus, it would be difficult to start anywhere else than with Heinrich Friedrich August Ruengling and his children. Heinrich was German, and his wife, Marie Salomé Juliar, was French.

The couple's seven sons and a daughter were born in Baraboo, Wisconsin. These "Ringling Brothers" have been called the "Kings of the Circus". It took many years of hard work before the family business could be called "The Greatest Show on Earth". Their nine team Wagon Show in 1884, according to IRS rules, had "trapeze, wire rope walking, trained ponies, dancing and singing". The original name was "The Ringling Brothers United Monster Shows, Great Double Circus, Royal European Menagerie, Museum, Caravan, and Congress of Trained Animals", By 1919, Ringling Brothers was the dominant circus across America with premiere acts and traveled in special private railcars. By 1929, they had acquired the Barnum & Bailey Circus, the Al G. Barnes Circus, the Buffalo Bill's Wild West Show, the Sells-Floto Circus, the John Robinson Circus, and the Hagenbeck-Wallace Circus.

The Ringling circus was noted for prohibiting profanity in front of patrons and prohibiting short-changing customers.

All seven brothers were Masonic brothers. Alfred Theodore Ringling (an accomplished juggler), John Nicholas Ringling, Albert Charles Ringling, Charles Edward Ringling, William Henry Otto Ringling, August George Ringling, and Henry William George Ringling were all Initiated, Passed, and Raised in Baraboo Lodge #34 of Baraboo, Wisconsin.

The town of Ringling, Montana, was named for John, who owned the White Sulphur Springs and Yellowstone Park Railway. The railway town of Ringling, Oklahoma, was named for the family's circus train.

For obvious reasons, their only sister, Ida Loraina Wilhelmina Ringling, was not a brother Freemason.

Bro. Vance Swift of Pythagoras Masonic Lodge #355 in New Albany, Indiana, was billed as "The World's Smallest

Mason". Swift was but twenty-six inches tall when he was Raised a Master Mason in 1943.

Casper H. Weis never measured over forty-two inches in height, but he spent his ninety-three years as a very big man.

His parents bore eight children in Morcheningen, Dutchy of Luxembourg, but only Casper and his sister, Martha, were *tiny* people. Casper was an accomplished watchmaker and violinist by his early twenties. That was when he was offered an opportunity to travel with a side-show, and travel he did; first in Austria and then Poland before performing in Russia. Czar Nicholas II was so impressed with Caspar's performance that he removed a large emerald ring from his finger and presented it to "the little watchmaker".

In 1895, Casper came to America. To perfect his English, he spent a year in New York City working during the day as a watchmaker and playing his child size violin in clubs during the evening.

Once he felt comfortable with his new language, he joined "The Coney Island Midget Village" as its bandleader. While with this troupe, he met a young Parisian girl by the name of Jeanne Douvain. Casper not only courted her, he had to woo Jeanne away from the Barnum and Bailey Circus where she was known as "Queen Mab, the Smallest Midget Actress in the World". Jeanne was only thirty-eight inches tall, and Casper was someone she could look up to. They were married in 1906 and in 1913 purchased a "retirement" mansion in Canton, Pennsylvania.

Casper was quite a businessman. He managed and appeared in numerous circus and vaudeville circuits with acts entitled: the Original Lilliputian Company, Hans Fritz & Company, the Katzenjammer Kids, the Kaptain & Kids, Mutt and Jeff Review, and the Midget Follies Company.

In Canton, Casper never fully retired as he had hoped. People from around the country would bring him watches and clocks for his skillful repair and to view the Weis' extensive collection of memorabilia. Disaster struck in 1951, when a fire swept through the mansion destroying his watch making tools and the couple's treasured mementos. For the last fourteen years of his life, Casper and Jeanne lived in an apartment provided to them by a Lodge brother, Robert Elliott.

Casper was a member of Lulu Temple Shrine of Philadelphia for over sixty years, a life member of Richard Vaux Masonic Lodge #384, the Jerusalem Royal Arch Chapter #3 of Philadelphia, the Scottish Rite, and the Commandery.

The Commandery dedicated June 21st as the Casper Weis Day because he was "The Shortest Knight (night)". But that honor actually belonged to John Bergert of Council Bluffs, Iowa, who is depicted in the accompanying photograph.

Reuben A. Steere didn't run away to join the circus, it came to him. As a young man, Steere was accustomed to the routine of farming and commissions from the occasional sale of farm equipment. Reuben's life changed when Fred Bunch met the farmer and "discovered, the Second Tom Thumb". Bunch ran a sideshow with the Stone & Murray's Circus.

Steere eventually grew to forty-four inches while he was with the George Bailey Circus. Later, he hired on with the Karl Stefan Bailey North American Circus.

He met and married Rebecca Ann Myers when she was with The Lilliputian Opera, after having left the G.G. Grady

Circus. The couple eventually tired of the constant travel and decided to settle down. Steere move the family back to Rhodes Island, where "Annie" ran a confectionary shop next door to Friendship Masonic Lodge #7. Reuben had a day job as the truant officer for the school district, where the kids were bigger than he was, and held the job of Lodge Tiler at night.

John Aasen was a big man in Freemasonry, even before he held any office. Bro. Aasen stood six inches over eight feet and weighed in at 536 pounds when the Third Degree of Masonry was conferred on him at Highland Park Lodge #382 in Los Angeles, California, by Grand Master Arthur S. Crites.

Fifteen-hundred visiting brethren attended the publized conferral. With that many craftsmen present, it was effortless for the Master to locate the dozen Fellowcraft that were necessary to assist Bro. Aasen through the ceremony, although not effortless for men assisting the giant candidate.

In keeping with the topic of this chapter, it should be noted that among Bro. Aasen's motion picture credits was his appearance in *The Circus*.

James Grover "The Texas Giant" Tarver was 8'5" tall during his twenty-six years of circus touring with Ringling Brothers. Circus patrons who paid to shake his hand received an embossed pot-metal 1 ½" ring as a memento. These rings have become collectible. Born in Franklin, Texas, he always appeared in a cowboy hat and high-heeled western boots. He appeared in only one movie, the 1917 forgettable *Jack and the Beanstalk*. James was typecast as the giant. He was a member of Alba Lodge #633 of Alba, Texas, a noble of Hella Shrine of Dallas, Texas, and a 32nd Degree Scottish Rite Mason.

The inspiration for the iconic Uncle Sam is said to be Daniel Rice. The first use of Uncle Sam was in 1816, seven years before Rice was born, but it was his portrayal of "Yankee Dan" in top-hat, red-and-white striped pants, and his tailored goatee that captured the imagination of mid-nineteenth century America and inspired the period's political cartoonists.

Rice was twenty-one before he ran off with the circus and created his clown persona. Rice was hailed as the first widely recognized American clown. Breaking the stylized mold of European diamond-clad harlequins and buffoonery clowns, Rice amassed a small fortune while commanding the unheard of sum of a thousand dollars a week in salary.

He ran for President in 1868, believing he could wrest the Republican nomination from Ulysses S. Grant based solely on his popularity. Stripped of his caricature image, Rice suffered personal ridicule and rejection that he had never experienced when performing as his alter-ego.

Bro. Rice was a member of Lake Erie Lodge #347 in Girard, Pennsylvania.

Karl Adrian Wettach was better known throughout his career as Grock. The famous Swiss clown was born in 1880 and achieved acclaim as an acrobat and musician before donning whiteface makeup, as a sad hapless clown.

The character of Grock was a failure at all he tried. If he sat in a chair, it collapsed. If he fetched a pail of water, the bucket had no bottom.

Besides his world recognition as "The King of Clowns", Bro. Wettach was the highest paid performer in the world, not just among clowns, but the highest among musicians and actors of the era.

He was only slightly less acclaimed for the 2,500 songs he composed, and his virtuosity with the two-dozen musical instruments he had mastered.

Bro. Wettach was a member of the Swiss Grand Lodge Alpina and the Grand Lodge in France. His home in Imperia, Italy, is now a clown and circus museum.

As a clown, Emmett Kelly was often compared to Wettach's character of Grock. Emmett Leo Kelly's clown persona of "Weary Willie" had a gentle sadness that lacked the outright slapstick of Grock. Like Bro. Wettach, Kelly was also a Freemason. His Craft Lodge was Sarasota Lodge #417 in his hometown of Sarasota, Florida. He was also a 32nd Degree Scottish Rite Mason. He toured with the Shrine Circus in 1957.

Besides his numerous motion picture roles, he was a headliner with Ringling Brothers, Barnum and Bailey Circus from 1942 through 1956. He was an "on field mascot" for the Brooklyn Dodgers.

His son, Emmett Kelly, Jr. reprised the beloved character of Weary Willie during his own clown career.

Born in the New York of the 1820s, Fayette L. "Yankee" Robinson was apprenticed to a shoemaker while still a child. He learned to read and studied the Bible. He soon discovered he had the gift, or art, of elocution and understanding peoples' desires. He taught dancing to ladies in the evenings and saved enough money to purchase a wagon and one horse. He built a traveling stage on the wagon frame and traveled the warm weather circuit performing biblical morality skits, saving lost souls, and collecting pocket change.

Again, he saved enough to expand and purchased a tiny circus. He bought a second small circus and combined them into a larger 175 horse circus. Robinson always wanted to expand and that was his downfall. He over-extended into a 225 horse circus and went bankrupt.

Ever the opportunist, he worked for the W.W. Cole Circus, the Sells Brothers Circus, and the Ringling Brothers

Circus. While working with Ringling Brothers, Robinson first revealed that he was a Mason. Strong Masons themselves, the Ringling Brothers entered into a deal with Robinson, backing The Yankee Robinson Ringling Brothers Great Double Show that toured the Midwest.

Robinson died while the circus train was in Jefferson, Iowa. The Masonic ring on his finger was the only proof ever located that he was a Freemason. But the ring was sufficient for the local Morning Star Lodge #159 to provide a Masonic burial. Circus friends erected a stone monument with Masonic symbols over his grave.

He was born William Claude Dukenfield in 1879 and was a professional juggler by age eleven in Norristown, Pennsylvania. Fortunately, we have proof of the youth's incredible juggling expertise from a handful of motion picture films. Young jugglers wanting to learn the art of cigar-box juggling need look no further than Dukenfield's singular performance as "The Great McGonigle", in the otherwise forgettable 1934 film *The Old Fashioned Way*.

We know this wise cracking juggler better by his stage name, W.C. Fields. This great vaudeville and film actor was a member of E. Coppee Mitchell Lodge #605 of Philadelphia, Pennsylvania.

Gerald Montgomery Blue was born Montgomery Bluefeather, but is better known as Monte Blue to the film-going public. This is due to his 283 movie and television appearances that spanned from 1915 until 1960. His best known role was that of Sheriff Ben Wade in the 1948 Humphrey Bogart movie *Key Largo*.

His distinctive features were a gift from his young Cherokee mother and older white father. Monte's father had fought with the Union during the Civil War and later rode with

Buffalo Bill Cody as a frontier scout. His father was killed in 1895, when Monte was eight. His widowed mother couldn't cope with the bullheaded youngster and admitted him to The Soldier's and Sailor's Orphans Home of Knightstown, Indiana.

Monte took hard labor jobs as a coal miner, cowhand, fire fighter, lumberjack, and semi-professional football player. His horsemanship skills earned him jobs with two circuses and that led to work with D.W. Griffith in the film *Birth of a Nation,* in which Monte was a stuntman on horseback.

He was a member of Utopia Lodge #537 of Los Angeles, California, and the famous 233 Club for Masonic Actors. As his acting career waned, he returned to circus life as an advance-man for the Hamid-Morton Shrine Circus.

He often boasted of performing Harry Houdini's airplane stunts in the 1919 film *The Grim Game* because Houdini, a fellow Freemason, was terrified of flying. Bro. Blue has a star on the illustrious Hollywood Walk of Fame.

Oscar Winner Ernest Borgnine was Raised in Abingdon Lodge #48 of Abingdon, Virginia, before affiliating with Hollywood Melrose Lodge #355 of Hollywood, California. Bro. Borgnine was active with Al Malaikah Shrine in Los Angeles and the Shrine Circus, as well as, being a 33rd Degree Mason in the Scottish Rite.

The Academy Award winning actor is noted for his tough-guy movie image, few know his early training was in classical theater. His first role was on Broadway in the comedy *Harvey.* From 1962 to 1966, he was the popular star of the farcical television comedy *McHale's Navy.*

Borgnine regularly participated incognito in the Annual-Spring Great Barraboo Wisconsin Circus Parade while in clown costume and clown makeup.

The diminutive Chester Conklin began his career as a Barnum and Bailey clown before getting slapstick work in Mack Sennett's Keystone studios.

Conklin is rumored to have created Charlie Chaplin's "The Tramp" concept and costume for the then unknown British actor. Whatever the truth, Chaplin did keep Conklin around for seven years.

He continued in comedic roles with Sunshine and Fox Studios, but it was his work with W.C. Fields at Paramount Pictures that earned him his star on the Hollywood Walk of Fame. Bro. Conklin was a member of University Lodge #394 in Inglewood, California.

Aside from a redheaded clown hawking hamburgers, probably no other clown is as well remembered as Freddie the Freeloader, as portrayed by Red Skelton. Born Richard Bernard Skelton in 1913, Red started performing at the age of twelve in minstrel shows, circuses, medicine shows, vaudeville and as comic relief between acts in burlesque carnival shows.

It was his repertoire of likeable characters on his television show that won the hearts of Americans: the inept Sheriff Deadeye, the country bumpkin Clem Kadiddlehopper, the not-so-honest real estate agent San Fernando Red, and the bum with a heart-of-gold, Freddie the Freeloader.

Bro. Skelton was a member of Vincennes Lodge # 1, in Vincennes, Indiana, a 33rd Degree Scottish Rite Mason, a York Rite Mason, and an Al Malaikah Shriner in Los Angeles.

William DeWolf Hopper started his career as a lawyer, but yearned for limelight. His stage debut in 1878 was less than auspicious as he lacked the characteristics common for the leading men of the day.

Hopper had been bald since childhood and at six-foot-five towered over fellow actors and actresses. As a result, he spent his career in farcical musicals.

Hopper's major claim to fame came not from his melodramatic buffoonery, but from his recitation of a single poem. Noted for his booming voice and elocution, Hopper performed Ernest Thayer's then unknown poem "Casey at the Bat", during a New York Giants game in 1888, and continued accepting requests for further recitations throughout his life.

He claimed to have performed the poem over 10,000 times; including on a 1906 Victor First Prize Record and in a short 1923 Phonofilm movie production.

His personal life was often as melodramatic as his stage performances. In addition to uncounted mistresses and children, he married six times. The most notable marriage being to the striking Elda Furry, better known to the public as Hollywood radio and newspaper gossip columnist, movie star, television actress, and dancer Hedda Hopper. They had one son, William, who achieved fame as the tall-blonde cigarette-smoking private detective, Paul Drake, on the successful *Perry Mason* television series.

Like many Broadway actors, Bro. Hopper was a member of Pacific Lodge #233 of New York City, New York. He was also a 32nd Degree Scottish Rite Mason and a Shriner at Mecca Shrine of the same city. Bro. Hopper's autobiography was titled, *Once a Clown, Always a Clown.*

Clyde Beatty was always fast to correct anyone who called him "America's Greatest Animal Tamer". As he was oft to point out, "If my lions and tigers are tamed, there is no act." The featured performances in his own Clyde Beatty Circus included not only trained lions and tigers, but also an expanded menagerie of leopards, cougars, and even hyenas.

His trademark dinner chair and whip were frequently insufficient in thwarting off real danger, as Beatty was in the hospital more than five-dozen times with injures as minor as fang bites to as serious as a skull-crushing two-week coma.

All of Bro. Beatty's Masonic affiliations were in Detroit, Michigan. He was a member of Craftsman Lodge #521, Royal Arch Masons Monroe Chapter #1, Knights Templar Damascus Commandery #42, and Moslem Shrine Temple. He was a frequent headliner in the worldwide tours of the Shrine Circus.

When one thinks of cowboys and circuses, *Buffalo Bill Cody's Wild West Show* instantly comes to mind. Few of us associate the famed film cowboy Tom Mix with the genre of circus. It was Tom's horsemanship and trick roping skills that won him national competitions and recognition in 1909, but it took him fourteen years of cow poking and traveling circus shows with the Sells-Floto Circus before he ventured onto the silver screen.

When offers of film roles ceased to flow his way, he toured with his own Tom Mix Circus and Wild West Show, to moderate success. His hero image on the big screen didn't translate well off-screen to this less than average height showman, even with his feet shod in his silver-trimmed high-heeled cowboy boots.

Like the "Singing Cowboys" Gene Autry and Roy Rogers, this rodeo cowboy was active in multiple branches of Masonry. Masons can become "Life Members" of their home Lodges by paying their dues for a number of years in advance. Although not a Life Member of his Lodge, Bro. Mix paid his dues to Utopia Lodge #527 of Los Angeles, California, ten years at a time. Like many Hollywood actors, he was a member of the 233 Club, Scottish Rite, and York Rite Masonry.

One of the most successful and well liked comedy duos of all time, Laurel and Hardy, has been mentioned in Lodge Trestleboard as fellow Freemasons. This is only half correct.

Norvell Hardy was a troublesome child for his widowed mother. He ran away from home to join a minstrel show, ran away from boarding school to join a vaudeville show, and ran away from a military college to sing in cabaret shows.

Norvell took his dad's name of Oliver throughout his vaudeville and movie career. He was ten years into his movie career when he was paired with Stanley Laurel, and the rest is history, as the saying goes. The public affectionately called the tie-twiddling big man by the nickname of "Ollie", but his friends and Masonic brothers of Solomon Lodge #20 of Jacksonville, Florida, knew him as "Babe".

The thinner half of the comedy duo, Arthur Stanley "Stan" Jefferson Laurel, was unable to attend Hardy's Masonic funeral due to illness, but made note of it in his personal correspondence. As to whether or not Laurel was a Freemason, he answered that question in a 1957 letter. "It was interesting to note that you are a Mason, a wonderful organization. My Dad was a 32nd degree member in the Scottish Order, for some reason I never became one."

Noted for understated slapstick, the duo was oft called the "Clowns of Comedy". Neither man ever worked in a traveling circus, except for an appearance on the silver screen.

In 1932, they appeared in a movie called *The Chimp*, where the bumbling twosome brings a circus to financial ruin. The premise of the film was simple. The owner of the circus discovered he didn't have sufficient funds to meet payroll. In lieu of cash payments, he parceled out his circus property to the performers. Ollie received a dancing ape named "Ethel", and Stan acquired a flea circus in a small box. The cinematic magic these two conjure up from such a simple premise defies description. If you have never watched the film, rent it.

Being that this author is an attorney, it is a horrifying thought as to the mirth and joy the world would have lost if Hardy had followed his mother's wishes and become a lawyer.

CHAPTER 9

BIRDS OF A FEATHER

Class lodges are sororities or fraternities that only accept candidates that belong to a defined group, trade, or social strata.

At its worse, a class lodge can result in displays of racial bigotry, snobbery, and parochial thinking.

At its best, it offers the exploration of diverse heterogeneous ideas addressing a single trade or interest, exemplifying the expression, "Two heads are better than one."

Operative Lodge #40 in Dumfries, Scotland, is a modern day class lodge that only accepts members who "have served an apprenticeship with a recognized trade within the building industry".

For nigh on to three-hundred years, Operative Lodge #150 of Aberdeen, Scotland, admitted only operative masons. The "Granite City", as Aberdeen is called, was founded by the guilds and trades associated with the nearby quarries.

When steamships became practical in the 1850s, the city began shipping both materials and master stonemasons to every point of the compass. Many brothers of Operative Lodge were seasonally employed in the New England region of America, especially around Barre, Vermont.

Sixty-four Aberdeen Masons helped build the Texas State Capitol Building in Austin in 1886. The men were imported due to a labor strike by local workmen.

During World War One, Aberdeen brothers braved German torpedoes to labor in America. One Lodge brother brought home a gift, a Master's apron from an American Lodge he attended. The apron is removed from its case once a year to be worn when Aberdeen's new Master is installed.

The most well-known structure built by Aberdeen Masonic brothers was London Bridge (the one that was moved to Lake Havasu City, Arizona, as a tourist attraction).

The tradition of admitting only operative masons as members began in May 1781. It came to an end in 1963. However, the Lodge continues to practice the traditional operative rituals in lieu of modern speculative rituals.

Griffith Griffith arrived in Placer County, California, in 1864 from Penrhyn, Wales, where he worked as a quarryman. He purchased quarry land in Placer and established the town of Penryn, dropping the "h" to make it easier to spell (at least that's what the City history says).

Griffith recognized the quarry's biotite granite as being excellent material for building foundations and support walls. To maximize his profits from these materials, he established a polishing works business alongside the quarry.

Seventeen operative masons, who were employed in the Penryn Granite Quarry, established Penrhyn Masonic Lodge #258 in 1879. The Masonic Temple was erected with ashlars hewn and squared from the quarry.

Penrhyn is the only California Lodge founded by Masons who were all operative masons.

Caledonian Railway Lodge #354 of Glasgow, Scotland, has operated since February 5, 1849. Its original Charter states, "The Lodge shall be composed entirely of Brethren connected with or in the employment of the Caledonian Railway Co. at the date of initiation, passing, raising or affiliation. ... The Lodge to be moveable and have power to meet at suitable places on the line of the Caledonian Railway, or such other Railways as may become part of the Caledonian, ... The Lodge to be ranked as a Metropolitan Lodge and under the immediate jurisdiction of the Grand Lodge in Edinburgh. ... No meetings to be held in any railway carriages, engine houses, booking offices, or other un-tieable (sic) fabric ... No meetings to be held out of Scotland."

Capital City Masonic Lodge #354 in St. Paul, Minnesota, began on April 7, 1895, as a "Railway Lodge". All its officers and almost all its charter members were employees of the Chicago, St. Paul & Omaha Railway Company. The brethren of the current Lodge represent an amalgam of the professions and occupations found in any modern community.

During the late 1800s and first half of the 1900s, Railway Lodges or Lodges that accommodated railway workers were a common practice. King David's Lodge #209 in San Luis Obispo, California, had available to such brothers, lodgings, a shower, and a monstrously heavy claw-foot cast-iron tub on the third floor above the Reception Hall and Ladies Lounge.

The Incorporated Society of Musicians Lodge #2881 meets at Freemasons Hall, Great Queen Street, London, England. When founded in 1902, its membership was restricted to professional musicians. Charles Ireland was the first non-musician to be admitted. A railway employee by trade and the nephew of a member, Bro. Ireland was initiated June 23, 1945, and served as Master in 1951.

Perhaps due to Bro. Ireland's contributions, the Lodge bylaws were amended September 17, 1960, to admit "(a)

Professional musicians, (b) Persons closely connected with the musical profession, and adherents (in whatever capacity) to the Art & Science of Music and (c) Near relatives of members of the lodge".

Today's membership includes singers, amateur musicians, music industry businessmen, music teachers, and computer engineers employed by sound studios.

Overseas Masonic Lodge #40 of Warwick, Rhode Island, is a classic class lodge. Overseas #40 is the only Military Lodge Chartered by The Grand Lodge of Rhode Island.

The entire membership of Overseas is composed of active military personnel, Honorably Discharged military veterans, or servicemen drilling with an Armed Services Reserve Unit. All of Overseas' Officers wear their military or former military uniforms during Lodge rituals, instead of traditional black tuxedos.

The annual "Venison Night" held each December or the annual paint ball competition of Civil Service Lodge #148 in Ottawa, Ontario, would appear to be enough to make the Lodge stand out in a book on Masonic trivia, but #148 has another claim-to-fame. Its officers and members "must be employees of the Civil Service of Canada or either branches of the Legislature."

The result has been a list of past officers and members from Civil Service Lodge that reads like a "Who's Who" of Canadian history.

When Civil Service Lodge was constituted back in 1861, its petition fee for membership was twenty dollars ($20) and the annual dues were three dollars ($3). That may not be much in our modern currency, but it was a healthy bit of coin out of the typical civil servant salary of only one hundred dollars a year ($100/year).

One of the most exclusive Masonic groups is The Society of Blue Friars. Membership is by invitation only and is limited to Masonic authors. Founded in 1932, the Society admitted its one-hundredth member in 2011. Growth is slow because the bylaws allow that, "One new Friar shall be appointed each year."

The bylaws provide a safety clause to prevent membership from becoming dangerously low, "Additional Friars may be appointed to fill vacancies caused by demise or resignation when the total membership is not over twenty."

The Society meets each February in the nation's capital. At the meeting, the newly inducted member is expected to deliver an oral presentation on his research paper addressing a topic related to Freemasonry.

The list of famous magicians who were Freemasons includes; Harry Keller, "The Dean of Magic", who performed for President Teddy Roosevelt and his family; Howard Thurston, the "King of Cards", who was more famous in his day than Houdini; Erik Weisz, better known by his stage name of Harry Houdini, "The Handcuff King"; and the two Harry Blackstones, both Senior and Junior. As a side note: Harry Blackstone Senior's original "Floating Light Bulb" is on display in the Smithsonian Institute.

The Invisible Lodge was founded in 1953, in New York, New York, by Brewerton H. Clarke, better known as "Sir Felix Korim". The entire membership of the Invisible Lodge consisted of performing magicians who were Masons.

During World War Two, Clarke worked for the US Army at Griffiss Air Force Base designing camouflage systems. This appears to have been a good position for a magician who designed his own disappearing illusions. Clarke's most famous deception being "The Cloak of Invisibility", in which he would drape a black cloak over his wife; the cloak would slowly turn transparent to show she had dematerialized, leaving nothing behind but her angel mist shape in the white gossamer fabric.

The Army made good use of another Freemason magician, Joseph McCloud "Jack" Gwynne. Gwynne was known as "The Aristocrat of Deception". He designed and built props for Houdini in 1925-1926. After Houdini's death, he toured under his own right. The most famous among his many illusions was one where he made a pyramid of seven glass bowls filled with water and live goldfish disappear. Jack was employed by the Army in its psychological warfare division, as well as, performing USO shows entertaining troops in Africa, Burma, China, Iran, and Italy.

The Invisible Lodge isn't chartered like a regular Lodge. This doesn't mean it exists because of some Freemasonry hocus-pocus. The Lodge exists more along the lines of a specialized Masonic club. It has more than eight-hundred members. An annual meeting is held at the Columbus Magi-Fest in Ohio. Smaller regional gatherings occur at magic conventions.

Instead of Masonic signs, grips, and words, magic tricks are used as a means of identification.

The Lodge's philanthropic endeavors involve performances at children's hospitals and group homes, where the performers magically levitate spirits and assistants.

With all the current public interest in both Masonry and magic, it is doubtful the Lodge will vanish in a puff of smoke.

CHAPTER 10

GENTLEMEN, COCK YOUR PISTOLS

Dueling was such a problem in early California, that in May of 1854, the Grand Lodge ruled that any brother killed in a duel was not entitled to a Masonic funeral, and any survivor would be expelled from the fraternity.

The Grand Lodge's ruling was not enough to prevent a Masonic duel from occurring three months later. Hilliard P. Dorsey had been the first Worshipful Master of Los Angeles Lodge #42. Ramsey Biven was a member of San Joaquin Lodge #19, who moved to Los Angeles in September of 1854.

Ill blood existed between the two men over property rights. One early September day while Dorsey was in the office of Dr. Mylis, Biven entered, drew a revolver, and fired at Dorsey from point blank range. Incredibly, he missed. Dorsey charged Biven and pinned him against a wall. The usually hot-headed Dorsey, much to the surprise of the witnesses present, refused the opportunity to shoot Biven and instead insisted that the matter be settled by a public duel.

What was Dorsey's motive? During the War with Mexico, Dorsey had been a Captain from Mississippi under Colonel Jefferson Davis. In the manner of many Southern military officers, Dorsey had fought in several duels.

The well-publicized duel was fought on September 23, 1854, using Dorsey's personal set of dueling pistols. Biven's skill as a marksman must have improved. The duel resulted in both men receiving grievous wounds. The Grand Lodge suspended both men and expelled Dorsey at its next regular session, noting, "... in a written communication to the Grand Secretary he (Dorsey) has acknowledged the facts as charged and declared that under similar circumstances he would do the same thing again, therefore be resolved, That said H.P. Dorsey be and he is hereby expelled from all the rights, benefits and privileges of Masonry."

The youngest daughter of William Wiley Rubottom, Pomona Lodge #246, was named Civility. She was the wife of Dorsey. In 1857, she took her five month old son, Kewen, with her and fled her husband's abuse. A Freemason neighbor got her safely to the home of her father, known locally as "Uncle Billy".

Accounts state that Dorsey "captured" his son from his father-in-law's home in El Monte and demanded that Civility return with him. Instead, she staked out their home, "re-captured" the boy, and again made her way to her father's home by the aid of local Freemasons.

Dorsey learned from a storekeeper named Cyrus Burdick that his wife and son were back with Uncle Billy. Before he left Burdick's store, Dorsey loaded his "brace of dueling pistols" and stuck them loosely in his belt.

Uncle Billy was no stranger to killing, as he was wanted for murder back in Arkansas. When Dorsey advanced with his pistols drawn, Uncle Billy discharged his double-barreled shotgun. The buckshot killed the expelled Past-Master.

Dorsey had fought in the Mexican War under the command of Colonel Kewen, a prominent Mason and lawyer, who went on to become California's first Attorney General. The Dorsey's son was named for the Colonel. Later, the boy survived an accidental poisoning that killed his step-father and went on to become a prominent Freemason.

If Dorsey had fired first, there might not be any opossums in California. The Rubottom family has claimed that Uncle Billy was responsible for turning two-pairs of imported Arkansas opossums loose in California in 1875, because he was upset that there were *"none of them critters"* in California.

Dr. Isaac Earl Featherston was the Edinburgh educated Surgeon Superintendent aboard the SS *Olympus* until May 1841, when it arrived in Wellington, New Zealand. In addition to his medical practice, he was also the Editor of the *Wellington Independent* and the First Superintendent of Wellington Province.

The New Zealand Company owned the *Olympus* and regularly transported people from England in an attempt to colonize Wellington into "A perfect English Society". That worked about as well as Uncle Billy and the opossums.

Colonel William Nathaniel Wakefield was the New Zealand Company's Principal Land Agent in the province.

Featherston and Wakefield were brothers in Freemasonry, but that is as close to fraternal relations as the two men ever came.

While Featherston's life in England had been on the straight and narrow as a medical student, Wakefield's complex life was the stuff of twists and various windings that make Hollywood screenwriters daydream of Oscars.

In 1825, Wakefield was betrothed to Miss Emily Sidney, but the marriage failed to take place because the groom and his brother were behind bars. The two men were charged with the abduction of a wealthy heiress. While released on bail, Wakefield took flight to Paris, France, where Emily joined him. She pleaded with him to return to England and marry, because she was three months pregnant, but he refused.

After their daughter was born, he returned to London, was arrested forthwith, and held at Lancaster Castle. Miss Sidney tragically died six months into Wakefield's three year sentence. Their infant was christened with her mother's given name, Emily, and cared for by Wakefield's sister, Catherine.

Although he was lacking in any military experience, Wakefield traveled to Portugal in 1832, to serve as a mercenary army Captain for the Emperor of Brazil, Dom Pedro. He barely survived the siege of Oporto due to his own ineptitude, but received medals nonetheless.

His next military stint was with the British Auxiliary Legion, where he fought in the First Carlist War on behalf of infant Queen Isabella II of Spain. He was promoted to Major on the basis of sheer survival. Both sides were known for their butchery by executing both prisoners and wounded men in the field. He bartered his re-enlistment for the rank of Colonel and a knighthood by Queen Isabella.

In 1837, he retrieved his daughter from London and headed for the fertile antipodal opportunities of New Zealand.

In 1846, he married the girl off to Edward William Stafford. Stafford was the son of Irish gentry who, having failed in his studies at Trinity College in Dublin, had been exiled to Nelson in the Tasman Region of New Zealand. The groom may have had the weaknesses of cards, women, and drink, but he was gentry. Later, he surprisingly redeemed himself by becoming the third Premier of New Zealand.

Things were looking good for Bro. Wakefield as the Principal Land Agent. That is until he read Bro. Featherston's editorial of March 25, 1847:

"Did those mud hovels scattered along the beach, or those wooden huts which appeared every here and there ... represent the City of Wellington? Where were the hundreds of acres of [quoting from the Company's marketing] 'fine fertile land which shall produce such astounding crops?' My own investment was not as promised, but a useless swamp worth nothing".

Wakefield believed he had been called a thief and demanded satisfaction. Seconds were "particulared" (designated), and the time and place was set in the suburb of Te Aro for the following day.

The two adversaries paced off, turned and Featherston fired, but failed to hit his target. Wakefield proclaimed that he "would not shoot a man who had seven daughters" and fired into the air.

This enraged Featherston, who demanded another shot, but was refused by both men's seconds, Bro. John Dorset and Bro. Francis Bell, who declared the matter resolved.

Bro. Featherston fathered two more children, his only sons, and later commented that the duel must have changed his luck with children. He died in 1876.

Bro. Wakefield had a heart attack the next year and died at only forty-five. According to newspapers, including Featherston's, his funeral was attended "by half of the citizens of Wellington", the Governor, and Masons from around the Province.

Virgil Earp and his brothers, Wyatt and Morgan, were frontier lawmen of questionable virtue when Virgil petitioned for membership in King Solomon Territorial Lodge #5 of Tombstone in the Arizona Territory in 1881. Disregarding the allegations of local corruption, prostitution, and larceny, the investigating committee returned a "full and favorable" report.

Nevertheless, several members of the Lodge blackballed Virgil. When these brothers later came forward, they claimed it wasn't Virgil's involvement in prostitution and corruption that prompted rejection. It was because he was a noted gambler.

Today, Lodges in Texas, Pennsylvania, and Wyoming hold fundraising raffles, a form of gambling, with prizes of rifles, shotguns, revolvers, and semi-automatic pistols. What would those Masons of 1881 Tombstone have thought?

"The Fremont Street Shootout" became known as *The Gunfight at O.K. Corral* when a movie of that name was released in 1957. The shootout began with what had the appearance of a group duel. The Earp brothers and Doc Holliday in one rank and the Clantons, the McLaurys and Billy Claiborne in an opposing rank only six to nine feet apart. After thirty-seconds of gunfire, three men lay dead. Disregarding witnesses who testified that Billy Clanton and the two McLaurys were surrendering when killed, Judge Wells Spicer cleared Virgil and his brothers of murder.

Who was Justice of the Peace Wells Spicer? He was the first Master of King Solomon, shared a common-wall second-story office in the famed Crystal Palace Saloon with the Earps, and had earlier in the year signed Virgil's petition for membership in King Solomon.

When Indiana became the nineteenth state in 1816, its capital was near the southern edge of the state in Corydon. It took another nine years for the capital to move north to Indianapolis. But our story occurred a year after Indiana statehood and shows that California wasn't the only state to have a problem with dueling Masons.

Masons gathered a convention in Corydon on December 3, 1817, to draft a constitution for a Grand Lodge of Indiana. At the time, all nine Lodges and the 195 Masons in the new state, except Harmony Lodge in Brookville, were chartered or Under Dispensation from the Grand Lodge of Kentucky. Harmony's Charter was from the Grand Lodge of Ohio.

Lawyer Alexander Buckner was elected Secretary of the Convention. The attendees agreed to form the new Grand Lodge and to elect Grand Officers on January 12, 1818. Buckner moved the site of the election to Madison for two reasons. The first was simple, that was where he lived with his mother and sisters. The second was political, there had been a bitter rivalry between Corydon and Madison as to which city should be the State Capital, and Buckner was a Madisonian.

Buckner was elected Grand Master, but his tenure was short-lived. By September he had pulled up stakes and emigrated from Indiana to Missouri, where in 1831, he became a pro-slavery United States Senator. He died during the devasting Asiatic cholera epidemic of 1833.

The reason for Buckner's departure from Indiana was said to stem from a duel with attorney Thomas Holdsworth Blake of Terra Haute, Indiana. The two men were opposing counsel in the case of Thomas Proctor. Proctor was charged with larceny of nine beaver pelts. Words were exchanged between the two attorneys that lead to the formal exchange of lead shot. The barbs of their words apparently did more damage than their marksmanship skills, both attorneys failed to strike flesh with their shots.

Blake went on to become a judge and later served in the US House of Representatives of the 20th Congress in 1827.

On September 28, 1897, Bro. Buckner's remains were re-buried in Cape Girardeau cemetery with Masonic honors performed by Grand Master J. Black of Indiana and Grand Officers of Missouri. An inscribed monument was erected on the spot overlooking the Mississippi River.

Buckner is the only Mason to have fought a duel while holding the office of Grand Master.

CHAPTER 11

GHOSTS OF THE PAST

The first Masonic funeral to be held in California was in Yerba Buena Cemetery in 1849. The deceased was a man whose identity was unknown to the assembled throng of Masons and curious onlookers. What had attracted the mass attendance was not the identity of the man, but the means by which it had been ascertained that he was a fraternal brother.

A description of the drowned brother's remains, as recovered from San Francisco Bay, was reprinted in the May 27, 1868, edition of the *Sacramento State Capitol Reporter*.

"Upon his body was found a silver mark of a Mark Master, upon which were engraved the initials of his name. Further investigation revealed to the beholders the most interesting exhibition of Masonic emblems that were ever drawn by the ingenuity of man on human skin. There is nothing in the history of Freemasonry equal to it.

"Beautifully dotted on his left arm, in red and blue ink, which time could not efface, there appeared the emblems of an Entered Apprentice: the Holy Bible, the Square and Compasses, the twenty-four-inch gauge, and the common gavel. There were also the Masonic pavement representing the ground floor of

King Solomon's temple, the indented tessel which surrounds it, and the blazing star in the centre.

"On his right arm were the square, and the level. There were also the five orders of architecture – the Tuscan, Doric, Ionic, Corinthian, and Composite.

"On removing the garments from his body, the trowel presented itself, with all the other tools of operative Masonry. Conspicuously on his breast were the Great Lights of Masonry. Over his heart was the pot of incense. On other parts of his person were the bee-hive, the Book of Constitutions, guarded by a Tyler's sword pointing to a naked heart, the all-seeing eye, the anchor and ark, the scythe, the forty-seventh problem of Euclid; the sun, moon, stars, and a comet; the three steps, emblematical of youth, manhood, and age. Admirably executed was the weeping virgin, reclining on a broken column, upon which lay the book of constitutions, in her left hand she held the pot of incense, the Masonic emblem of a pure heart, and in her uplifted right hand a sprig of acacia, the beautiful emblem of the immortality of the soul. Immediately beneath her stood winged Time with his scythe by his side 'which cuts the brittle threat of life', and the hour glass at his feet, which is ever reminding us that 'our lives are drawing to a close.'

"It was a spectacle such as Masons never saw before, and in all probability may never witness again. The brother's name was never known."

Another account states that each brother in the concourse of attendees "deposited a branchlet of evergreen" (acacia) into the grave.

Buried in the Oak Lawn Cemetery of Jordan Station on the shores of Lake Ontario is another sailor-brother whose identity is known only to the Great Architect.

In 1877, Jordan Station was but a mere hamlet. What advantage it lacked in magnitude of population, was compensated for by a blessing of nature, Jordan Harbour was a deep cut glacial bay. Nearby was St. Catherines, Ontario, Canada and Temple Lodge #296. Temple had received its Masonic Charter in 1873. It is believed that the brethren of Temple Lodge pitched in financially for the unknown brother's funeral, but their records were destroyed in an 1895 fire. The anonymous sailor's tombstone tells his story best:

HERE
LIETH THE REMAINS
OF
AN UNKNOWN BROTHER
WHOSE BODY WAS WASHED ASHORE
NEAR THE RESIDENCE OF
ABRAM MARTIN ESQ LOUTH
ON 20TH APRIL 1877
THIS TOMBSTONE IS ERECTED TO SHOW THAT
WHILE DECEASED HAD ONLY ON HIS PERSON
CERTAIN SYMBOLS TO DISTINGUISH HIM AS
A FREEMASON YET WERE THEY SUFFICIENT
TO SECURE FOR THE REMAINS FRATERNAL
SYMPATHY AND CHRISTIAN SEPULTURE
DEAD VOICELESS BATTERED TEMPEST TOSSED
A STRANGER FRIENDLESS AND UNKNOWN
THE WAVE GAVE UP ITS DEAD. A BROTHER
CAME AND SAW. AND RAISED ABOVE
HIS LONELY HEAD THIS SCULPTURED STONE
THE MYSTIC POINTS OF FELLOWSHIP PREVAIL
DEATH'S GAVEL CANNOT BREAK THAT SACRED TIE
GAINST LIGHT THE POWERS OF NIGHT CAN
NAUGHT PREVAIL. TO LIVE IN HEARTS WE LEAVE
BEHIND IS NOT TO DIE

In 1996, Heritage Lodge #730 sponsored a new gravestone of granite as the original had been toppled and was fading from erosion and neglect. The original marker is on display in the museum of Niagara Lodge #2 GRC in Niagara-On-The-Lake, Canada.

Bro. Samuel Horowitz was elected Master of Ionic Lodge #520 of Los Angeles in 1930, and was looking forward to his forthcoming installation. However, fate intervened and Bro. Horowitz was struck seriously ill. With their beloved brother about to succumb, the brethren contacted the Grand Master of California, who granted Ionic a special dispensation.

With the Ionic officers gathered in his hospital room, Bro. Horowitz was installed as Master of their Lodge. His term of service lasted but seven hours before he traveled onward to that land from whose bourne no traveler returns.

It would be remarkable for a man to have even one unique Masonic distinction. Bro. Angelo Soliman exceeded the probability with several unique peculiarities. He was born in Africa in 1720 or 1721 and sold as a wee child into slavery. Working in aristocratic European households, the young boy perfected a fluency in several languages and became a master chess player.

He entered the service of Prince Johann George Lobkowitz of Naples in 1732 and that of Prince Joseph Wenzel of Liechtenstein in 1753. Soliman traveled extensively with both Princes throughout Italy, France, Germany, and most of Europe.

On behalf of the Holy Roman Emperor Joseph II, he accompanied Wenzel in September 1760 as a proxy escort for Joseph II's future bride, Isabella of Parma. In Schönbrunn Palace there still hangs a painting where Soliman is clearly portrayed in the bride's entourage as she entered Vienna.

Bro. Soliman was the first African native to enter the Craft. He was Initiated a Freemason in 1781, in the prestigious

Zur Wahren Eintracht or True Harmony Lodge. Soliman sat in Lodge with Wolfgang Amadeus Mozart, who joined in 1784. Soliman married a widowed baroness with the blessing of the Imperial Court and the social elite of True Harmony. He became Master and Grand Master and instituted the practice of reading scientific and academic papers during Lodge meetings, including papers on newly discovered theories of geometry.

Unfortunately, this remarkable brother is most noted for the bizarre posthumous fate he met in 1796. Over the protests of Soliman's daughter and his Masonic brothers, Emperor Franz II had a taxidermist flay and stuff Bro. Soliman's body. His denigrated remains were then garbed in a loincloth, shell necklaces, and a plumage embellished crown. The Emperor was proud of depicting this "noble savage" as the ruler of three other mummified black men included in a tableau of stuffed African wildlife. This scene in the Imperial Natural History Museum was made open to public viewing.

On Halloween 1848, fate again intervened in Bro. Soliman's travels when a nihilistic incendiary of the Austrian Revolution hurled a firebomb into the Palace. The resulting conflagration cremated the remarkable brother's residuum, but left intact his singular legacy.

There is a Masonic ghost town in California, or rather, Masonic is a ghost town in California. The town of Masonic was named by Joseph Green for his affiliation with the fraternity of Freemasons.

What was once a roistering camp of rough and tumble sourdoughs (experienced miners), rowdy tenderfeet (inexperienced newcomers), loose women (doesn't need defining), and highwaymen and pikeys (thieves) in the 1860s is now occupied by an occasional flock of baaing sheep, tongue-flicking lizards, and a "moaning" ghost.

During the 19th century, this Mono County canyon town northeast of Bridgeport, California, swelled to a population of over a thousand. Little remains as evidentiary testimony to the heyday of activity around its Pittsburg-Liberty Mine. The mine was abandoned a century ago. The rare visitor can still see the original tram system used for hauling ore from the mine to the mill, but it is now used by Mother Nature for making iron-oxide, better known as rust, amid the remaining handful of dilapidated cabins and shanties.

In 1908, well after the mine had ceased production, the body of one of the partners, Mr. J. Phillips, was discovered at the bottom of a mine shaft. Foul play and treachery were believed to have been involved in Mr. Phillips having been given the shaft. To this day, the town's rare visitors, except for the sheep and lizards, report hearing Phillip's ghost moaning from the depths of the mine. It is unknown if his grief is for his loss of life or loss of gold.

In 1774, George Washington (Yep, the one on our money) sold Ferry Farm, his childhood home, to his friend Hugh Mercer. The two men met on the Pennsylvanian frontier, during their escapades in the French and Indian War.

Mercer had soldiered as a surgeon in Scotland for the exiled "Bonnie Prince Charles". Hunted as a rebel by the Brits, he fled to America, settling near what is now Mercersburg, Pennsylvania, to practice medicine.

In 1767, the doctor became a member of Fredericksburg Masonic Lodge and later sat in the East as Master when George Washington and James Monroe were members.

After the Declaration of Independence was penned and war broke out, Mercer became a brigadier general in the Continental Army, again fighting the Redcoats.

In a skirmish prior to the Battle of Princeton, Mercer had his horse shot out from under him. He fought hand-to-hand, suffering repeated bayonet and saber wounds. He refused his men's entreaties to leave the field of battle even though mortally wounded with a broken bayonet impaled in his body. His men propped him against the trunk of a white oak, where he urged them to stand their ground until Washington arrived and drove the British off the field of battle.

The "Mercer Oak" is an element in the county seal for Mercer County, New Jersey. But the oak is not where his ghost haunts. Fredericksburg Lodge #4 was organized in 1752. Among the 270 graves within their cemetery's sandstone walls is where visitors report hearing Bro. Mercer's Scottish brogue lamenting never having returned to his beloved bonnie highland hills.

A mile out to sea, off the northern Oregon coast, rests the Tillamook Rock Lighthouse. Legend has it that the men manning "Terrible Tilly" were "ghost-house keepers" as well as lighthouse keepers.

Station keepers where hoisted to the inaccessible rock by a derrick, while suspended in a breeches buoy. The derrick was one of only two ways onto the craggy rock. The other method involved a death-defying leap from a sea-tossed boat onto the barnacle encrusted slimy boulders.

John R. Trewavas was both a Master Mason and an operative mason. He had experience in the similar construction of a lighthouse on Wolf Rock near Land's End in England. While Bro. Trewavas and an assistant named Cherry were attempting the leap to Tillamook in 1879, Trewavas was swept into the turbulent sea. Cherry bravely, or fool-heartedly, leapt in after him in a futile attempt to save the distressed brother.

Cherry was rescued by the crew of the tender, but Trewavas's body never surfaced.

During two years of challenging construction at the lighthouse, Bro. Trewavas's drowning was the sole death. More than one stouthearted keeper has reported that Trewavas's disquieting cries could oft be heard echoing up the winding staircase toward the lantern room.

The Dollar Line launched the SS *President Hoover* in 1931. She was designed to carry 988 passengers and a crew of 385. Like her namesake, the poor liner saw her share of troubles. On August 30, 1937, she was mistaken for a Japanese vessel and bombed by the Chinese Air Force, while loading refugees in the Yangtze River. Six crewmen survived with serious wounds, one didn't, but he was not the first crewman to die on deck of the *Hoover*.

Charles "Chips" H. McCoy was the "Ship Carpenter" for the *Hoover* in 1935. With the dawn of Monday, May 27, the liner was five days out from Yokohama with a destination of her home port in San Francisco, when McCoy became violently ill. Bro. McCoy of Berkeley Lodge #33 in Berkeley, California, was unaware that before the Sun was at Meridian height (noontime), he would travel no more.

Robert Dollar, the steamship line's founder, had also founded the Masonic Lodge in Bracebridge, California. When the Hoover's Chief Officer, Bro. Carl W. Hawkins of Whatcom Lodge #151 in Bellingham, Washington, reported McCoy's death and requested instructions, a radio telegraph message was received from the home office, "Burial at sea, with Masonic service."

The crew and passengers were canvassed for members of the Craft. On May 29 at four in the afternoon, the Captain, Bro. Fred E. Anderson, stopped the *Hoover's* engines. Over fifty brothers formed a procession to the quarterdeck, where Bro. McCoy's body was placed on the grating to the ship's starboard (right side) gangway. One brother crewman donated his white lambskin apron. A first-class passenger donated a pair of white gloves. These were sewn into the canvas shroud along with Brother McCoy's earthly remains.

Hawkins conducted the service, the ship's orchestra provided appropriate music, and a crewman, Bro. Henry E. Johnson of Evergreen Lodge #259 in Riverside, California, sang several solos before the departed brother was consigned to the vast sepulcher of the deep. The ship hove to for an hour before resuming speed and course.

Captain Anderson's simple evening log entry read, "Voyage from Yohohama, bound for San Francisco, May 29, 1935, 2000 hrs; Buried at sea with Masonic Honors at 1600 hrs today, ship's carpenter Chas McCoy. Position, 29° 22' N, 177° 16' W."

A handsome young fireman by the name of John Edward Cameron was buried in the Masonic Cemetery near Central City, Colorado, just off Chase Gulch and Old Tram Road in 1887. But, the ghost that haunts the Masonic Cemetery is not that of Bro. John.

A large four sided monolith pillar marking his grave is inscribed "John E., Dearly Beloved Son of R. & C. Cameron, Died Nov 1, 1887, Aged 28 years." His mother, Catherine, died in 1912 and his father, Robert, preceded him in 1880. Their names and information, as well as, a square and compass adorn the other sides of the monument.

Twice a year, once on the anniversary of his death, November first, and again on April fifth, a date without peculiar characteristic, a beautiful young woman in a period black satin mourning-dress would appear and place columbine flowers on Bro. Cameron's grave.

One year, a dozen town folk gathered to confront the ethereal woman to inquire if April fifth was to have been the date of her wedding to John. Legend has it that as the group approached the woman, she "vanished through their midst" as a spectral mist, leaving nothing behind, but the columbines and a chill up the spines of the nosy town gossips.

Some wives are called "Masonic Widows" because their husbands spend so much time at Lodge meetings. Miles McGuigan's wife was one such woman, because Miles just didn't know when to leave the Lodge. He stayed in his Lodge for over a hundred years.

McGuigan was born in Bodny, County Tyrone, Ireland. In 1797, he enlisted with the 81st Regiment of Loyal Lincoln Volunteers, serving as a drummer boy under the Duke of Wellington in the Peninsular War. He survived being shot in both legs, and continued his military service in both Italy and Spain before his regiment was moved to Kingston, Canada, for service in the War of 1812.

Miles was discharged after the war and deeded a hundred acres of Canadian land for his term of service. Taking advantage of the proposed building of the Rideau Canal in 1826, he filled his pockets with more than two coins by selling his inland property and purchasing riparian plots on Ontario's Rideau River.

Further land speculations turned a sizeable return on his investments. In 1839, he married "The Leahy Widow" and moved onto her farm, a Crown Grant property. The farm maintained a cemetery known as The McGuigan Cemetery, which does not contain brother Miles for whom it is named.

The reader may wonder what became of Miles McGuigan's earthly remains. Per his request, his body was dissected and his bones placed in the Lodge of which he was an active member, viz, Merrickville Masonic Lodge #55, located in the St. Lawrence District of Ontario, Canada. His testamentary desire was that his remains would be made use of during Third Degree Canadian rituals. The brethren of Merrickville carried out his wishes until 1959, when the remains were cremated in a conflagration that destroyed part of the Lodge.

Stephen "One Eye" Girard was America's first multi-millionaire, seven times over. It is only natural that his funeral of December 31, 1831, in Philadelphia's German Holy Trinity Roman Catholic Church would attract a large group of mourners, especially in light of the invitation to the public printed in local papers.

When a procession of Pennsylvania's Grand Lodge, Philadelphia's Mayor, and four-hundred other Masons arrived wearing (as reported in the next day's newspapers) "sheepskin aprons and regalia, officers in collars and jewels", the clergy of the church walked out. The visiting Masons stepped forward to fill the void and performed a Masonic service for their departed brother.

Girard had been born in France and baptized as a child in the Catholic Church, but had left the fold. His sister claimed that on his deathbed, he repented his apostasy, and a priest was summoned, only to arrive after Stephan had died. The sister appealed to Bishop Kendrick, who permitted the funeral at Holy Trinity and wrote of the incident in his diary:

> "The body of Stephan Girard was brought with much funeral pomp, attended by many Free Masons marching in procession in scarfs and ornaments, as a tribute of respect to their deceased companion, to the church of the Holy Trinity. When therefore, I saw these enter the Church to have funeral rites gone through, no priest assisting, I ordered the body taken away for burial."

Bro. Girard bequeathed only $140,000 to his stunned relatives. He left $800,000 to build a canal and maintain "Delaware Avenue". He left over $6 million to establish a school and a college to care for and educate orphan boys. The relatives sued to nullify the philanthropic will, and lost.

In December 1850, Girard College and the City of Philadelphia made arrangements for the disinterment of his body from Holy Trinity and to have his sarcophagus re-entombed in a polished marble vault within the newly constructed main building of Girard College.

The relatives sued to prevent the proposed entombment and lost, again. The re-entombment was performed by Grand Lodge officers, and Judge Joseph Chandler delivered the eulogy, "His memory is cherished by his brethren and the Masonic fund, which bears the name of Stephen Girard Charity Fund, has done untold good to the recipients."

American Revolutionary Brigadier General George Rogers Clark is frequently over-shadowed by his younger brother, William Clark of The Lewis and Clark Expedition fame.

But, it's this senior brother who holds the Masonic distinction of being buried twice, or more precisely, who was buried in bits and pieces.

In 1809, Clark suffered a mild stroke and fell into his fireplace. The severe burns to his leg necessitated its amputation. At the General's insistence, two drummers and two fifers played as the surgeons performed the operation.

Past Master George requested his severed limb receive a Masonic funeral, and his fraternal brothers of Abraham Lodge #8 in Middleton, Kentucky, complied with his request.

The rest of the General didn't receive the same honor until nine years later.

When Benjamin Franklin died in 1790, the Grand Lodge of Pennsylvania refused to permit him a Masonic funeral. Franklin was a Past Grand Master of Pennsylvania and Past Master of Loge des Neuf Soeurs (Nine Sisters Lodge) in Paris, France. At the time of his death, the Grand Lodge of Pennsylvania had changed its affiliation from the Grand Lodge of England (the Moderns) to their rival, the Antient Grand Lodge of England. Franklin's prior affiliations were considered clandestine by the Antients. The acidulous schism between the two Grand Lodges was healed with a unification in 1813.

On April 19, 1906, the Grand Lodge of Pennsylvania convened at Franklin's grave in the cemetery of Philadelphia's Christ Church and perform a belated memorial service for their most celebrated member.

Well known Masonic author Harold Van Buren Voorhis' fraternal affiliations included memberships in 21 national, 3 state, and 11 local appendant and concordant Masonic bodies. These were in addition to his term as Master of Mystic Brotherhood Lodge #21, of Red Bank, New Jersey, in 1937.

W.Bro. Voorhis had a lifelong passion for amateur radio, beginning in 1915 as a charter member of the Radio League of America. His "ham" radio experience gave him years of practice with tape recordings.

He put this experience to good use by recording his own Masonic funeral for both a church service and a graveside service. He also included the renderings of his own prayers.

With a voice from beyond the grave, W. Bro Voorhis conducted his own funeral services in 1983.

CHAPTER 12

IT'S A WHOLE DIFFERENT GAME

The Masonic Lodge in the small railroad town of What Cheer, Iowa, would on occasion have more Masons attending rituals than the entire official population of the town.

The brethren of What Cheer Lodge completed their three-story brick building in 1894. Architect J.J. Gordineer's Romanesque design has withstood the test of time, and the building is on the National Historical Registry.

Even though the Lodge structure displays three-stories of windows on its outside front façade, there are only two-stories within. The top floor is the Lodge Room, and the bottom "two-stories" were built as an opera house; hence the derivation of the building's name, the "What Cheer Masonic Opera House".

The Opera House brought much needed income to the Lodge and provided entertainment for the public, who came from as far as four-hundred miles away to attend events. This was partly accomplished by means of the railway connections.

The high banked tiers of seats in the Opera House made it easy for the audience to see into the orchestra pit and view the entire fifty-foot stage. In its early years, the Lodge hosted vaudeville acts, revival preachers, repertory theater performances, politicians, comedic social commentators, musical virtuosos, singers, magicians, jugglers, trick-rope artists, traveling dance companies, the occasional minstrel show, and even an opera.

The inclusion of the name Opera House in the names of Eastern seaboard and Midwest Masonic Lodges occurred with some regularity between the late 1800s and early 1900s. The large open floor space of the Lodge Room was ideal for a variety of events and amusements. Lodge Rooms were used for roller-skating events, dances, speeches, political debates, and even sporting events, as the next account illustrates.

The Masonic Temple Hall in Trenton, New Jersey, was the site of the first professional basketball game on November 7, 1896. The third floor of the Lodge was converted for the purpose by installing bleachers, nets, and backstops. Seating in the bleachers was at a premium, and attendees were charged accordingly, twenty-five cents for the bleachers and fifteen cents for standing room outside of the cage.

Yes, there was a wire cage to keep the brawling players separated from the audience, who would burn visiting players with cigars. It took until World War One for the "Trenton Monkey Cage" to disappear from basketball. Now you know where the term "Cagers" came from in basketball.

Fred Cooper was the captain of the Trentons and had organized the game. For his effort, he was paid a dollar more than the fifteen dollars received by each of the other players. The players definitely earned their money, as early professional basketball was at least as bruising as rugby. Players were expected to continue playing with broken noses on blood splattered floors. The tallest of Trenton's five man team was their rebounder, Gus Endebrock, at five-foot-nine.

Two years later, the National Basketball League held their first season of professional basketball. Cooper's Trentons won the national title for the first two years.

In that groundbreaking game of 1896, the local Trenton team beat the visitors from Brooklyn by the lopsided score of 16 to 1.

There was a splendid abundance of pomp and celebration on July 15, 1884, when the cornerstone of the Masonic Temple Hall was laid by the Masons of Trenton, New Jersey. The architect was one of Trenton's native sons, William A. Poland, who had not envisioned his four-story block-long structure ever being used for caged basketball gladiatorial contests with blood splattered floors.

Until the late twentieth century, it was a common practice for Temple Board of Trustees or Hall Association Directors to finance the purchase of realty and the construction of large Masonic Centers by selling public shares of ownership.

Unbeknownst to the brethren of Trenton Lodge, the Trenton Banking Company had engaged in a stealth campaign to acquire a majority of the shares. By 1916, the Bank had the necessary shares to demolish the historic Hall in favor of the construction of a more commercially lucrative bank and office building.

James "Jimmy" H. McClure liked to play lawn tennis, when he wasn't tap dancing. He was an excellent dancer and appeared on stage with movie star Dick Powell.

It began to rain one day during a game of lawn tennis, when Jimmy was fifteen. Jimmy went inside the club house and learned to play table tennis. Two years later, the gracefully agile youngster was the 1934 American Ping-Pong Association's National Champion.

Parker Brothers owned the American (but not English or European) trademark and rights to the name "Ping Pong", and marketed a line of paddles, balls, and tables for the developing sport. They immediately knew the handsome youth was a marketing gold mine and wanted to sign the boy to an endorsement deal. Jimmy negotiated an unheard of "percentage of the profits as royalties", in lieu of the "flat up-front fee" that was standard in the industry.

McClure went on to garner four gold medals and two bronze medals in World Championships and six United States Championship tournaments.

Parker Brothers sponsored Jimmy on international tours to Europe, Japan, and China. He traveled extensively in the United States giving exhibitions and promoting the sport.

Jimmy was a member of Oriental Lodge #500 of Indianapolis, Indiana. During his travels, he would often engage in a bit of charity work by putting on fund raising events at Lodges near his exhibitions or tournaments. Every Lodge Room was large enough to accommodate a ping pong table and spectators to his demonstrations of nimble dexterity with a paddle and fleet footwork.

The marble and glazed terra-cotta Masonic Temple in Fort Greene, Brooklyn, New York, was designed by renowned architect James Monroe Hewlett in 1909. By 1912, it was the home to thirty-five local Masonic Lodges.

The 1200 seat concert hall on the ground floor is quadruple height. Through the decades, the Masons have kept current with the changing trends in entertainment. Their auditorium has been the progressive scene of vaudeville acts, rock-n-roll concert performances, and professional women's boxing matches. Talk about rolling with the punches.

CHAPTER 13

CHIPS FROM THE QUARRY

Siegmund Salzmann was born in 1869 in Budapest, Hungary, but spent most of his life in Vienna, Austria. He was a member of the historic *Freimaurerloge Zur wahren Eintracht* (True Harmony Freemason Lodge) in Vienna. During World War Two, he fled to Zurich, to escape Nazi persecution.

Of the many books Salzmann authored, he is most noted for two dissimilar international best sellers. Both have been translated into over a dozen languages, both have been made into movies, both have been the subject of college courses, and neither was published under the author's real name.

The first of the two was his pornographic fictional autobiographical memoir of a Viennese courtesan, *Josephine Mutzenbacher*. Its topics are no less shocking today than they were when it was first published in 1906.

The other novel was published under the pseudonym of Felix Salten in 1923. It has been called the "First Environmentalist Novel". Salzmann wrote the novel for adults, but the story has been become a children's classic in picture book, stage, motion picture, cartoon, and ballet adaptations. We know *Eine Lebensgeschichte aus dem Walde* better by the name of the orphaned *chevreuil* or male Roe Deer in Bro. Salzmann's story, *Bambi*.

One of the first things a man encounters on entering a Lodge of Freemasons is the representation of a pair of pillars that stood in King Solomon's Temple, and the representation is wrong.

Atop the pillars in the modern Lodge are two spheres. One is a globe of the Earth depicting its geopolitical borders. The problem is that in King Solomon's time, there was no knowledge of the United States, Canada, Mexico, New Zealand, Antarctica, China, Japan, Hawaii, North America, South America, etc. To the Hebrews of King Solomon's day, the Earth was flat and not spherical.

The second sphere is of the celestial sky and depicts stars that were only discovered after the 1876 invention of catadioptric (reflecting) telescopes with Mangin (concaved) mirrors.

What is the form (geometric shape) of a Masonic Lodge? Most people will answer, "A rectangle." But the correct answer is, "an oblong square".

I know that term sounds like an oxymoron. How can an object be both a square and oblong?

The answer lies in the relatively obsolete geometric use of the word "square". In ancient stonemasonry, a square was any object that was composed of right-angles. Thus, the two shapes we currently call a square and a rectangle were both squares under this old definition. So, how did early stonemasons know which type of square was to be used? If all four sides of the right-angled parallelogram were of equal length, it was called a "perfect square". If the length exceeded the width, it was called an "oblong square".

Many of us read Bro. Sir Walter Scott's novel *Ivanhoe* in junior high. In the story, Wilfred of Ivanhoe describes the tournament grounds for a jousting bout: "The ground, as if fashioned on purpose for the martial display which was intended, sloped gradually down on all sides to a level bottom, which was enclosed for the lists with strong palisades, forming a space of a quarter mile in length, and about half as broad. The form of the enclosure was an *oblong square, ...*"

Poindexter and Orr Cattle Live Stock Company registered the first cattle brand in Montana. It bore the design of a Masonic Square and Compass.

William Crosby Orr was born in Ireland in 1829. His family arrived in America when he was four. He apprenticed as a carriage maker in Mississippi before moving out West. In 1856, he formed a partnership with Philip H. Poindexter. They purchased over 40,000 acres of Montana Territory, raised shorthorn cattle, sheep, (Percheron, Norman, and Clydesdale) draft horses, and operated exorbitantly profitable butcher shops in the mining districts of Idaho and Montana.

Orr was a member of Dillon Lodge #30, Dillon Chapter #8, St. Elmo Commandery #7, Bagdad Temple Shrine, and the Order of Eastern Star, all in Butte, Montana. In 1894, Orr was High Priest of the Grand Chapter.

Poindexter belonged to the same Lodge, Chapter, and Commandery. Poindexter's wife, Mary E. Sappington, nee Baxter, holds the dubious distinction of planting the first wild dandelions in Montana.

While on the subject of the Wild West, the widower father of John and Nathan Tracy demonstrated his love for his two sons in a most unusual way. Knowing he was about to die, he bequeathed his boys, along with his farm, and cattle, to Eastland Masonic Lodge #467 of Texas, in his 1884 will. The brethren of the Lodge must have done well with the youngsters, for Nathan became the Grand Commander of Knights Templar of Texas in 1932.

Draisines came in many forms. The earliest looked like spidery one-man velocipedes (sort of an adult bicycle) with flanged metal wheels that rolled along railroad tracks.

When motorcars became popular, people converted everything from Model-T Fords to police cars to ride the rails. Next to come along were the Freemont Speeders, which resembled a cube the size of the front third of a Volkswagen microbus. In between the velocipedes and the speeders were the pump-trolleys or pump-cars that silent film comedians seemed always to procure when being chased by inept law enforcement or railway security agents.

In the early 1900s, Bro. Carl Brown, of El Centro Lodge #384 in California, worked for the Southern Pacific Railroad as the Station Agent in Calexico. Bro. Adolph Shenk also lived in Calexico. Brown had free use of a pump-car. The first

Monday of each month, Shenk would join Brown at a Calexico siding and roll the car onto the tracks. The two men would pick up brothers who, when not helping to pump the contraption along, could sit on the car's two side benches.

Bro. Brown's not picking up brothers of his Odd Fellows Lodge wasn't because he thought less of them. The I.O.O.F. #397 met on Thursdays, and there was conflicting railway traffic on Thursday nights.

Prior to 1895, each US Postmaster was permitted to design and make the hand stamps used to cancel letters at his individual post office. It was common for Freemason postmasters to create cancellation stamps depicting a square and compass, Masonic working tools, officers' jewels, or York Rite and Scottish Rite symbols.

Modern philatelists prize envelopes bearing postage stamps adorned with these unique cancellations as part of their collections.

Daintree Lodge #2938 was formed in 1902 by military personnel at Liu Kung Tao Island and on ships in Britain's Chinese Northern Fleet (The Peiyang Fleet). The men had been dispatched to stem the "plague" of pirate attacks along China's southern coastline.

In 1939, the Japanese invaded the naval base at Wei Hai Wei, China, and the Lodge's warrant was in danger of being captured. Their Senior Warden, Bro. R. H. Lackey, took the warrant to Singapore before smuggling it to Hong Kong aboard an Allied submarine.

On December 7, 1941, the Japanese attacked Pearl Harbor, Hawaii, and by the end of the month had seized Hong Kong and razed the city's Masonic Hall.

Bro. Mohamed Nemazee, a citizen of Iran and a member of Zetland Lodge #525, searched the remains of the Hong Kong Masonic Hall. Daintree's regalia boxes had been vandalized by the Japanese, who had scattered its contents about the floor. Despite the threat of death if captured with Masonic items, Nemazee secured the warrant, minute books, and regalia, before hiding them under a military hospital on Bowen Road, in a cavity under the hospital's foundation.

By 1947, the surviving members of Daintree had scattered to places far flung from China. To prevent its now retrieved warrant from being surrendered to Grand Lodge, brothers serving in the area of Fareham, England, (near Portsmouth) resurrected the Lodge there. At the age of 87, Capt. Daintree, for whom the Lodge was named, was present for the ceremonies. In 1970, the Lodge moved to its current location in Botley.

Referring back to the Iranian doctor, in 1948, Bro. Nemazee formed the Iran Foundation in New York. Donating $10 million of his family fortune, he built the Nemazee Hospital, Nemazee Nursing School, Nemazee Vocational School, and the Shiraz Water Works in Shiraz, Iran. Later, he was a member of the Shah's Cabinet when Iran was a close ally of the United States.

The allusions to operative work in Masonic Lodges focuses on buildings of quarried stone, but one Lodge in Canada has a history of building with grains of sand.

Beaches Lodge #474 in Toronto was built in 1905, in the usual architectual manner.

In recent years, their charity work has expanded to a competition with a dozen other District Lodges on the shore of Ashbridge's Bay for an Annual Sandcastle Building Competition. The event is all in good fun (except for their rivalry with Doric Lodge) and for a charitable cause. Of course, there is a cherished trophy to the winners, plus ice cream and food for all.

When examining the religions of antiquity from Egypt or the Orient, the Greeks or the Norse, Leviticus or Matthew, we discover some incarnation of *The Golden Rule*. Freemasons of every sect and opinion hold it in such high esteem that they have named their Lodges for it.

Golden Rule Lodge # 5	Stanstead, Quebec, Canada
Golden Rule Lodge # 16	Knightstown, Indiana
Golden Rule Lodge # 24	Rochester, Iowa
Golden Rule Lodge # 32	Pense, Saskatchewan
Golden Rule Lodge # 32	Putney, Vermont
Golden Rule Lodge # 77	Hinsdale, New Hampshire
Golden Rule Lodge # 90	Topeka, Kansas

Golden Rule Lodge # 126   Cambellford, Ontario
Golden Rule Lodge # 147   Nyssa, Oregon
Golden Rule Lodge # 159   Ann Arbor, Michigan
Golden Rule Lodge # 235   Hoboken, New Jersey
Golden Rule Lodge # 236   Allen, Nebraska
Golden Rule Lodge # 345   Covington, Kentucky
Golden Rule Lodge # 361   Hearne, Texas
Golden Rule Lodge # 409   Gravenburnt, Ontario
Golden Rule Lodge # 479   San Jose, California
Golden Rule Lodge # 616   Omaha, Arkansas
Golden Rule Lodge # 726   Chicago, Illinois
Golden Rule Lodge # 748   Philadelphia, Pennsylvania
Golden Rule Lodge # 770   New York City, New York
Golden Rule Lodge # 1261   London, England
Golden Rule Lodge # 1261   Willard, Ohio

The Grand Lodge of the State of Israel was formed on October 20, 1953. Israel has more foreign language Lodges represented within its jurisdiction than any other Grand Lodge in the world. Besides Hebrew, there are Lodges that conduct their rituals and business in nine other languages: Arabic, English, French, German, Hungarian, Romanian, Russian, Spanish, and Turkish.

The fact that Arabic is one of the ten languages, and used in four Israeli Lodges, may come as a surprise to Masons elsewhere around the globe, but not to Nadim Mansour, the Grand Master of the Grand Lodge of the State of Israel, who took office on February 25, 2011.

Mansour is a Palestinian Arab born in Akko, what the Templar Crusaders called the City of Acre, north of Haifa. Mansour, a Greek Orthodox Christian, became a member of Lodge Akko #36 on St. Patrick's Day in 1971, and is a 33rd Degree Scottish Rite Mason.

A headline for news bulletins at the time, could have read, "A BROTHER SAVES A LODGE".

In 1977, the Administration of President Jimmy Carter was willing to concede all United States' property within the Canal Zone, both public and private, to the Panamanian government. Pleas were presented to the US State Department to exempt Sojourners Masonic Lodge, but the State Department refused.

Sojourners had been granted a dispensation to form a Lodge in Cristobal in September 1912. The Panamanian government had previously agreed that the Lodge property would never be transferred to the government, a fact non-Mason President Carter was refusing to honor.

Sojourners Lodge was constituted on January 18, 1913, by the Grand Lodge of Massachusetts. There were 190 charter members, composed of Master Masons from forty of the forty-eight states (including Arizona which had been added less than a year before), and Masons from four foreign jurisdictions. Sojourners' peak membership was 4,036 brethren in 1962.

Senator Robert Dole, (a Brother of Russell Lodge #177 in Russell, Kansas, Senate Majority Leader, and the Republican Presidential Candidate in 1996), announced his intentions of introducing an amendment to the Treaty on behalf of Sojourners. A mere four days before the Senate was to vote on the Treaty and the amendment, Panamanian "President" General Omar Torrijos issued a guarantee:

"We recognize the validity of the title now held by the Sojourner's Lodge of Ancient Free and Accepted Masons. ... The entry into force of the Panama Canal Treaty of 1977 will not in any way impair the validity of this title."

Ultimately, it was Torrijos's guarantee that caused the Carter Administration to back-off, and the Treaty was passed.

As of 2010, Sojourners Lodge is still under the auspices of The Grand Lodge of Massachusetts. In 2010, the Right Worshipful John B. Bamber was its "District Grand Master - Panama".

The smallest Lodge in Ontario, Canada, wasn't formed because of the English Masons or the French Masons in the area. Its existence is due to immigrants from Iceland, who were never members of the Lodge.

Once upon a time, 352 Icelanders settled in a tiny hamlet called Kinmount for a mere two years. They came to construct the Victoria Railway connecting the cities of Haliburton and Lindsay.

In 1875, they moved to Nyja Island, which they called New Iceland. The island is located in Manitoba, on the western shore of Lake Winnipeg. They chose the land because it was ideal for cultivating and had an abundance of grasshoppers and fish (you read that right, grasshoppers). Their descendants now form the largest Icelandic community outside of Iceland.

During their two years in Kinmount, the town more than tripled in population, businesses, and construction of buildings. With the business growth and availability of the railroad, the town continued to expand.

As to Kinmount's Masonic history, Somerville Lodge #451 began in 1901 without a Lodge Hall. Meetings were held on the second floor of A.Y. Hopkins's home on Dickson Street. The brethren purchased its current white wood-framed Lodge from the Baptist Church in 1914.

Ontario is cold in the winter, and their meetings always end early. This tradition of promptness is less a product of Masonic punctuality than it is for lack of plumbing, electricity, and the fact that the wood stove is in the West, the greatest distance from the Worshipful Master's cold feet.

With only as many members as there are chapters in Deuteronomy (thirty-four), the brethren of Somerville are the smallest Lodge in Canada.

The 2010 film "*The King's Speech*" was great drama and won an Academy Award as Best Picture. But in terms of Masonic history, it failed to mention the fraternal relationship between King George VI and his speech therapist, Lionel George Logue.

Logue was a member of St. George's Lodge #6 in his native Western Australia. After being Raised a Master Mason in 1908, he served as Steward, Inner Guard, Junior Deacon, Senior Deacon, Junior Warden, Senior Warden, and Master. Upon moving to England, he taught at the Royal Masonic School for Boys, a charity established in 1798 for Masonic orphans.

Before he became King George VI and before he became the Duke of York, His Highness Prince Albert Frederick Arthur George of York was a Freemason. Navy Lodge #2612 Initiated Prince Albert in December 1919. Household Brigade Lodge #2614 had Initiated his older brother, Prince Edward, in May of that same year. The grandfather of these brothers and future kings, King Edward VII, had been the first Master of Navy Lodge. Following in his grandfather's footsteps, Albert became Master of Navy Lodge in 1921. Albert was active in Masonry his entire adult life. When he became King, he resigned his title as Grand Master and assumed the title of Past Grand Master as he visited Lodges across England.

When Logue began treatment of Albert in 1926, he noticed the Duke had particular trouble pronouncing words starting with a "Hard C" or "K" sound, but only in public speaking, not during Masonic ritual. Albert would stammer through a phrase like, "King of England", in a radio delivery, but easily flow over words like, "King Solomon", within a

Lodge lecture. Logue developed exercises designed to relax and pace Albert's delivery during public presentations.

When his older brother abdicated on December 11, 1936, in order to marry Bessie Wallis Simpson, Albert became King George VI. Of the meeting with his brother on the day of abdication, Albert wrote in his diary, "On entering the room, I bowed to him as King. When David (Edward's birth name) and I said goodbye, we kissed, *parted as Freemasons*, and he bowed to me as his King."

Names associated with King Solomon's Temple have been popular choices by Freemasons for Masonic Lodges over the centuries, as evidenced by the number which have included "Jerusalem".

Jerusalem Lodge #1	Napa, California
Jerusalem Lodge #4	Westmoreland, New Hampshire
Jerusalem Lodge # 9	Henderson, Kentucky
Jerusalem Lodge #16	Petersburg, Virginia
Jerusalem Lodge #19	Hartford, Ohio
Jerusalem Lodge #26	Plainfield, New Jersey
Jerusalem Lodge #31	East Bowmanville, Ontario,
Jerusalem Lodge #44	Clerkenwell, England
Jerusalem Lodge #49	Ridgefield, Connecticut
Jerusalem Lodge #62	Oregon City, Oregon
Jerusalem Lodge #84	Tel Aviv, Israel
Jerusalem Lodge #91	Rome, Italy
Jerusalem Lodge #95	Hookerton, North Carolina
Jerusalem Lodge #96	Ahoskie, North Carolina
Jerusalem Lodge #99	Clinton, Indiana
Jerusalem Lodge #104	Keene, New Hampshire
Jerusalem Lodge #115	Winnett, Montana
Jerusalem Lodge #197	London, England
Jerusalem Lodge #315	Jerico Springs, Missouri
Jerusalem Lodge #506	Philadelphia, Pennsylvania
Jerusalem Lodge #686	Bristol, UK

Jerusalem Lodge #909   Paris, France
Jerusalem Lodge #3000 District of Columbia
Jerusalem Temple #90   Aurora, Illinois
Jerusalem Temple #721 Cornwall, New York

During the conferral of the Masonic Degrees, a brother is said to have *traveled*. In our daily travels and commuting, we should all give thanks to the practical ingenuity of Bro. Edward N. Hines.

Hines was a printer by trade, a student of road construction as a hobby, and an advocate of concrete roads as a passion. In his profession as a printer, he published the nation's first *Tourbook* for travelers in 1893.

From 1906 through 1938, Hines was elected to the Wayne County, Michigan, Road Commission. He sought and received the backing of Henry Ford for the construction of concrete surfaced roadways. In 1909, he got his wish and the first mile of concrete road in the world was laid on Woodward Avenue between Mile Six Road and Mile Seven Road.

Hines also instituted snow removal from city streets as an innovative safety measure.

Hines was a member of Ashlar Lodge #91 of Detroit, Michigan. He is best remembered by travelers for an invention in 1911, the painting of white lines down the center of roadways as a means to prevent deadly head-on collisions.

Hector Kilbourne, AKA Kilbourn, was born in Simsbury, Connecticut, to Col. James Kilbourne and Lucy Fitch. James moved the family west to Ohio in 1801. He was a US Congressman from March 4, 1813-March 3, 1817.

As the eldest of eight children, Hector learned surveying from his father. In 1818, Hector joined a group of men planning to build a town in western Indian Territory.

Hector surveyed the chosen area and platted the proposed city of Sandusky, Ohio. His plat design was for a city that would eventually cover seventy-two square blocks and would have the appearance of an open Bible with Columbus Avenue being the center spine.

Overlaid on this open Bible design was the shape of a Masonic Square and Compass. Central Avenue represented the left arm of the Compass. Huron Avenue represented the right arm of the compass. Poplar Street represented the left leg of the Square. Elm Street represented the right leg of the square.

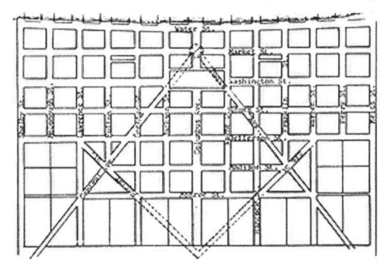

Besides being a surveyor and the town's postmaster, Bro. Kilbourne was also the first Master of Science Lodge #50 when it was chartered in Sandusky in 1819.

There was money to be made from California gold when Lewis Fuller Jones moved his family west, more money than he could earn as a wet-behind-the-ears Allegany lawyer. Upon reaching the gold fields, he took a job as a mining company chemist. In 1863, he was elected Judge in Mariposa County and held that post until entering private legal practice in 1865.

In 1867, Andrew M. Swaney was a widower and owner of the Mariposa Gazette. Mrs. Adelia Seale was the "charming and social" wife of the notable James W. Seale. Mrs. Seale was also an adulteress with widower Swaney. When James Seale was found murdered by poisoning with prussic acid, suspicion focused on the lovers. Charges were filed when Swaney was found to possess not only prussic acid, but also, books about prussic acid poisoning. Jones defended Swaney during the three week trial that resulted in a hung jury.

The retrial garnered so much local and national attention that the venue was moved from Mariposa to a larger courtroom in Stockton. The second trial was glorified in sensationalized daily newspaper accounts for readers up and down the Pacific Coast and as far east as the Atlantic seaboard. Like the first trial, the second ended with a hung jury. When the prosecutors elected not to pursue a third trial, the widow Seale married the widower. Members of the community were outraged at Jones for helping the lovers escape justice.

A year later, Jones petitioned Mariposa Masonic Lodge #23 for membership and was rejected. Clearly, someone in the Lodge had not forgiven him for his role in the trials.

Jones took a year to mend social fences by entertaining dinner guests with his virtuoso skills with the violin and flute before he reapplied to the Lodge. The second time, he was accepted and eventually elected by the Mariposa brethren as their Worshipful Master, not once, not twice, but nineteen consecutive times.

During the yellow fever epidemic of 1878, little Walter Carey Wilcox of New Orleans lost both of his parents. Friends put the small boy aboard a train bound for Sacramento, California, where his widowed grandmother lived. When he arrived in Sacramento, the railroad personnel took him to the Freemasons because the lad had a cardboard tag tied through a buttonhole on his coat commending him to the care of "any worthy Masons", stating the child was the orphan of a Mason.

By chance, the Grand Lodge of California was conducting their Annual Communication when the boy was deposited at their doorstep. The Grand Lodge adopted the child to their care, authorizing twenty-five dollars a month for his necessities, and the Grand Treasurer was appointed his guardian.

Seventeen years later, the Sublime Degree of Master Mason was conferred on Walter. He was a member of Oakland Lodge #188, but the ritual was conducted not by the local officers, but by the officers of Grand Lodge, and attended by visitors from across the state of California.

The American Legion is a patriotic service organization for veterans. The national organization serves veterans through local posts. In 1965, three posts in Chicago, Illinois, had memberships that were composed entirely by Master Masons. All three posts had names associated with Freemasonry: Square Post #232, Theodore Roosevelt Post #627, and Trowel Post #160. Posts #232 and #627 still exist.

During the ill-fated Braddock Campaign of 1755, the British attempted to capture the French fort of Duquesne in what is modern day Pittsburg, Pennsylvania.

As was the practice during the French and Indian War, the British forces carried Masonic regalia in "Lodge Chests" and had Grand Lodge warrants for "Military Lodges" that traveled with the troops instead of having a fixed building. Due to the fortunes of war, or misfortunes of war, Lodge officers frequently needed to be replaced.

Enter the short story of John Crockwell. He was a Fellowcraft when surviving brethren asked him to assume the post of "genitor". Believing his services were worth more than merely the "honour of the post", Bro. Crockwell agreed to accept the position on terms that he receive, "the third degree, fifty cents per night, and *a drink of toddy."* The Lodge accepted his terms, including the drink of toddy per meeting.

There is widespread, but not categorical, belief that Napoleon Bonaparte was Initiated into Freemasonry in June 1798 while on the Isle of Malta, possibly in the Army Philadephe Lodge. By July, he had reached Egypt and records there establish that he was received in Egypt as a Mason. No records exist of his ever receiving any Degrees beyond being Initiated. However, his interest in Freemasonry obviously continued as he appointed his four brothers to sundry Fraternal positions. His appointments included: Joseph as Grand Master of the Grand Orient of France, Lucien to the Grand Orient of France, Louis as Deputy Grand Master, and Jerome as Grand Master of the Grand Orient of Westphalia.

In the days of Capital Ships under canvas sail, a Letter of Marque and Reprisal was similar to fictional British Secret Agent James Bond's "Double-O, License to Kill". The fact that it was licensed piracy bothered neither issuing governments nor ship's crew.

The practice was so commonplace that shipbuilders purposely designed vessels ideally suited to the business of sailing under a Letter of Marque, and this style of ship took on the name of that document. Unlike privateers, which were sleek and fast with armament for staving off an attack, Letter of Marque were heavy square-rigged vessels designed to hold purloined cargo seized after boarding.

Between 1737 and 1779, two Letter of Marque vessels, named by their owners as the *Freemason* and the *Master Mason*, plundered the eastern seaboard.

In September 1779, Captain Benjamin Boden had set the *Freemason's* helm for Martinico from Marblehead Bay. Alas, the two masted brigantine's six guns and lumbering speed were no match for the British privateer's mounted sixteen guns. The British easily boarded the *Freemason* and captured her crew.

Capt. Boden, Thomas Cloutman, and "a small boy" were left on board under command of the British prize crew. The remainder of the *Freemason's* crew was placed in shackles aboard the privateer. Robert Wormsted, the *Freemason's* first mate, managed to escape from his shackles, free the rest of his men, and capture his captors.

When the shocked skeleton crew of British aboard the *Freemason* saw their own ship bearing down on them prepared to do battle, there was little they could do, but to hoist a white flag of surrender.

After depositing the privateers to prison and selling the spoils of their capture, Wormsted headed toward Massachusetts. The man had pressed his luck too far and was captured again, where he lost all.

The *Freemason* returned to Marblehead Bay where on September 30, 1779, it caught fire while at lying at anchor. She was destroyed when the fire burned through to her magazines of gunpowder. Buildings around the harbor and several ships were destroyed by the massive explosion.

Captain Boden went on to fight in the War of 1812, where he was again captured by the British. He was thrown into Dartmoor Prison for the war's duration.

The cornerstone for the Grand Lodge of Washington, D.C., was laid in 1907, with President and Masonic brother Theodore Roosevelt assisting. The outside façade of the building is decorated with symbols associated with the art of stonemasonry and the male only organization housed within.

The building still stands at 1250 New York Avenue NW with most of the original stone artwork, but it no longer is home to a Masonic Grand Lodge. Since 1987, the building has housed the National Museum of Women in the Arts.

Between 1787 and 1813, it was common practice for English merchants and cities to mint their own low value tokens or coins. The reason was one of avarice, not the greed of the merchants, but of the Royal Treasurer.

The Royal Treasurer was paid on the value of coins he minted, not on the number of coins minted by the Treasury. This gave the Royal Treasurer every reason to mint high value coins, and no reason for minting pennies, half-pennies, and farthings. To fill the needs of commerce, provisional tokens were privately minted by merchants, but could only be redeemed locally.

James Sketchley was an auctioneer, printer, and bookseller in Birmingham, England, who needed such low-value coinage. He minted a copper half-penny in 1794. The front of the coin depicted a commemoration of the Prince of Wales becoming the Grand Master of England in November 1790.

The reverse side bore an image of Cupid inside a triangle with an all-seeing-eye, the letter "G", a plumb, and a trowel. Around the triangle read, "Wisdom, Strength, & Beauty". These are words found on the pedestals in the East, West, and South of a Blue Lodge.

Around the outside rim was the Latin legend, *sit lux et lux fuit* or "Let there be light, and there was light".

Bro. Sketchley was Master of St. Paul's Lodge and Secretary of the Provincial Grand Lodge of Warwickshire from 1790 to 1792. Beside the coins, he is most well-known for inventing the street and house numbering system that he used in printing the first public directory of Bristol in 1775. Prior to his numbering system, houses were named for the owner, the builder, or a descriptive feature.

Acquiring a Sketchley Masonic coin today will cost you more than its half-penny face value.

When Simon Michael Meachan became a member of Old Denstonian Lodge #5490 of Denstone, Uttoxeter, England, (near Nottingham) in January 2006, he wore his grandfather's apron from 1889. He later discovered that his grandfather had gone bankrupt in 1896 and had been dropped from Zetland Lodge #852 for non-payment of dues. A delegation of Old Denstonian brothers accompanied Bro. Meachan to Zetland's April 2006 Stated Meeting, where the grandfather's 110 year old debt was paid off in open Lodge, enabling the grandson to wear the apron with renewed pride.

Three sitting Kings have been active members of American Masonic Lodges during their reign, all in Hawaii.
King Kamehameha IV
King Kamehameha V
King David Kalākaua

In 1922, the Third Degree of Masonry was conferred by Granger Lodge #677 of Granger, Texas, on the newly elected Bishop of the Methodist Episcopal Church South. The reader might expect a large turnout of Methodist Masons at a Degree conferral on their Bishop. But, the exceptional attendance was by Masons of many denominations and had more to do with the candidate's name, than his title: Rev. Hiram Abiff Boaz.

CHAPTER 14

THE HALLS OF JUSTICE

In 2010, the Honourable Madam Justice Maisonville of the Supreme Court of British Columbia, ruled on an application by Eva Notburga Marita Sydel regarding the appeal of the former dentist's conviction on nine counts of tax evasion. The convictions stemmed from charges of failing to report business income of $765,890 over a period of four years.

Sydel acted as her own attorney, which is about as wise as acting as her own dentist. The Supreme Court examined her several contentions:

One being that Sydel was a "Natural Person" and could not be convicted because a "Taxpayer" is an "Artificial Person".

Another being that her conviction was the result of a Freemason conspiracy, for which she had several theories that are best illustrated by the actual words of the Court:

"Ms. Sydel pointed to this in support of her Freemason conspiracy point. Kirby McAllister (a witness called by the Defense) deposed that he was a magician and had learned of hand movements to communicate during the course of his career, and while not professing to know the 'sign language' of Freemasonry, he deposed 'I have also learned that there is sign language carried out through the use of hand gestures and other bodily movements that is used by members of the Freemason fraternity, although I do not profess to know the sign language of Freemasonry.' He further deposed that during the course of the bail hearing of the plaintiff, 'I observed both Judge Paul Meyers and Richard Olney engaged in non-verbal communication through the use of a (sic) hand gestures and head movements.' ..."

"...the colours of the new British Columbia government logo are blue and gold which... are colours that are typically associated with Freemasonry ..."

"...the federal government's telephone numbers in Vancouver have the digits 666 in them. She submitted that 666 is the sign of the beast and is a number frequently associated with Freemasonry."

Fortunately, the Court avoided pointing out that by the dentist's argument, the *Gospel of Mark* could be construed as a Freemason conspiracy, because it is composed of 666 verses (London Edition of the King James Bible).

Instead, the Honourable Madam Justice succinctly ruled, "I dismiss the applicant's application." Apparently, the dentist's Freemason conspiracy accusations failed to have any teeth.

In 1425 A.D., Henry VI of England issued a decree that, *"Masons shall not confederate in Chapters and Congregations."* So the Masons changed the name of their gatherings to Halls and Lodges. A remnant of the old use is still found in York Rite Masonry where Royal Arch Masons still meet in Chapters.

One former Illinois Masonic brother sued the Lodge that had expelled him in 1877, for the return of his dues. The Supreme Court of Illinois ruled in *Robinson v. Yates City*

Lodge that an expelled member of a Masonic Lodge is not legally entitled to the return of fees paid. It held that Robinson had voluntarily paid his fees, knowing full well the terms of the provisions under which the Lodge could expel him. Furthermore, that under the rules and regulations of the fraternity, the payment of the fees did not constitute the creation of a contract. There being no contract, *ipso facto*, there was no breach of contract

The Supreme Court of Kansas heard an appeal in 1958 on a conviction of charges that read, "(Turner and other defendants) did willfully and unlawfully wear, exhibit, display and use for the purpose of misleading and confusing the public, a name, badge, button, decoration, charm, emblem, rosette and other insignia of the Prince Hall Grand Lodge of Kansas and Jurisdiction F. and A.M., ... while the said (Defendants) were not members of nor entitled to use and wear the same ..."

In affirming the convictions, the Kansas court relied on a ruling from the Supreme Court of Indiana in 1909, stating:

"The case of Hammer v. State (citations) is perhaps the leading case on the subject. There the defendant was charged with unlawfully wearing the badge and emblem adopted by an incorporated secret society of the state, he at the time not being a member of the society. He ... contended, among other things, that the law under which the prosecution was had was violative of the fourteenth amendment to the constitution. In rejecting this contention it was held that no constitutional privileges or immunities are denied a citizen by a statute forbidding him to wear the badge of a secret society of which he is not a member, nor are exclusive privileges unlawfully conferred by such legislation, and that the legislature may under its police power pass such legislation. In the course of the opinion it was said: "It can scarcely be urged that the right to wear a badge or emblem of a society of which a person is not a member is a right conferred by the Constitution or laws of the United States. The statute confers no right, exemption or privilege on any class or individual to do a thing denied to others as of common right, except it may be said negatively to authorize one who is a member of the society to wear a badge if he chooses, but prevents all who are not members from doing so. The Constitution and laws of the United States do not furnish, nor guarantee such right, nor can a person under them claim that right as a privilege, or that he shall be immune from regulation by the State, so far as the federal Constitution is concerned. It is simply the denial by the State, under its police power, of a claim of a right by appellant. It is the negation of a claim, and is a matter that concerns the State only. ... It is a matter of common knowledge that the membership in most, if not all, societies or organizations, whether secret or otherwise, is the result of fitness and selection, which give members standing and character, at least among their fellows, and to a greater or lesser degree with the public and he who wears a badge or emblem of the order or society without being a member holds himself out to the public and to actual members as guilty of a false personation. It is of itself a deceit and a false pretense, and its object could be nothing else than deception, with possibly ulterior motives.... and the object of the statute was the prevention of this species of fraud, not only in the interest of the members of the society, but of the public at large, who might be deceived through their good opinion of the society and its members. ...”

Between 1810 and 1834, hollow-ground straight-razors made of "silver steel" were manufactured in Sheffield, England, that were imprinted with the Masonic square and compass by a host of artisans.

In 1845, T. Archer of Sheffield manufactured one of the widest of straight-razors. The blades were 1 3/8 inches wide and etched with a variety of Masonic symbols.

Wade & Butcher Company of Sheffield produced Quarter-Hollow Wedge straight-razors in the 1800s with acid etched elaborate Masonic symbols. Some of their razors had inlaid gold Masonic emblems.

Simple stamped Masonic designs embellished the razors produced by Taylor.

Gilbert Brothers of Sheffield produced a bone handled Masonic straight-razor in 1852.

John Barber's straight-razors had a square-and-compass incised on the tang.

Lest it appear that only England was involved in the Masonic razor craze, Sandvik & Bessemer & Stal of Sweden also produced such razors in the mid-1800s.

This cornucopia of razors is an example of people using Masonic emblems for commercial exploitation, and it didn't stop with razors. The square-and-compass popped-up on ginger beer (sorry, bad pun) in the 1880s line of Davis & Son of Manchester and W.S. Haysworth of Preston, England; bars of soap in Pennsylvania; and the 1864 cattle brand of the Poindexter and Orr of the Montana Territory discussed on page 115 in this book.

In 1871, an American miller attempted to use the square and compass as a logo for his brand of flour, and a lawsuit was commenced against him. Although there was no trademark protection as such, the court found that the "square and compasses" was so clearly identified with Freemasonry that the miller was prohibited from using the symbol.

The American Commissioner of Patents ruled in 1872 that the square and compass emblem could not be used in any trademark or trade name for commercial purposes. Like leavened flour, the issue kept rising.

The Commissioner of Patents was General Mortimer Dormer Leggett in 1873. He ruled *In the Matter of John F. Tolle* that, "The square and compass is a well-known Masonic emblem of established signification, of which it cannot be divested so as to be used as a trade-mark."

Six years later, the issue was more than just a logo, when Acting Commissioner Doolittle came to a similar finding against trademarking the word "Masonic". "The word *'Masonic'* is objectionable as a trade-mark for the reason that it is not sufficiently arbitrary. Its employment might not lead to actual deception, especially among the Masonic order, but it would have that tendency."

In 1921, the Supreme Court of Nebraska addressed the issue of whether or not Freemasonry is a religion. In the case of *Scottish Rite Building Company v. Lancaster County et al* decided on April 20th of that year, Justice C. Dorsey wrote for the majority in finding that Masonry is not a religion:

"The true interpretation of the Masonic attitude in that respect (religion) is that no religious test at all is applied as a condition of membership. The guiding thought is not religion but religious toleration. The order simply exacts of its members that they shall not be atheists and deny the existence of any God or Supreme Being. Each member is encouraged to pay due reverence to his own God, the Deity prescribed by his own religion and to obey those precepts of human conduct, which, while taught by all religions prevalent in civilized society, do not appertain to the mysteries or doctrines of any religion, as such, but are common to all. The Masonic Fraternity, in other words, refrains from intruding into the field of religion and confines itself to the teaching of morality and duty to one's fellow men, which make better men and better citizens.

"The distinction is clear between such ethical teachings and the doctrines of religion. ... A fraternity, however, broad enough to take in and cover with its mantle Christian, Moslem, and Jew, without requiring either to renounce his religion, is not a religious organization, although its member may join in prayer, which in the case of each, is a petition addressed to his own Deity."

In the latter half of the 19th century, the US Internal Revenue Service permitted companies selling patent medicines, playing cards, matches, and canned fruit to design

their own tax stamps and to furnish the printing dies to the IRS Commissioner. This was essentially a form of free advertising for the companies.

The stamps for two Chicago manufacturers of "percussion matches" incorporated a Masonic Square and Compass into the designs of their 1877 tax stamps. One was Henry A. Clark and the other was Charles S. Hale. The two companies were thought to be related because of the similarity of the designs. Because it was required that these stamps be torn or destroyed when the consumer opened the package, they are quite rare and highly collectible.

CHAPTER 15

BROTHERS AT ARMS

The first recorded incident of a brother being saved by giving the Masonic Grand Hailing Sign of distress was on June 27, 1743. It occurred during the six-hour Battle of Dettingen, in Bavaria, during the War of Austrian Succession.

The Allies were called the Pragmatic Army because England had signed the Pragmatic Sanction of 1713 recognizing Maria Theresa as the Archduchess of Austria. King George II led the English Hanoverians into combat. This was the last battle where a British monarch led such an assault.

The French troops, under the command of Marshal De Noailles attacked, were repulsed, and lost the engagement.

During a failed cavalry charge ordered by Duc de Grammont, a French officer had his horse shot out from under him. The hapless officer's leg was trapped beneath his horse as an English dragoon raised a sword to administer the *coup de grâce*. Fearing the worse, the French officer gave the Grand Hailing Sign. Much to his relief, the dragoon stopped the advance, dismounted, helped disengage his leg, gave him a drink of wine from a canteen, and bound his wound.

The Englishman explained that as a Mason, he owed a duty to his King and country, and could not release the French brother. He escorted his prisoner back to headquarters, where the Frenchman was treated with kindness until the diplomatic cartel arrived to exchange prisoners.

During the War of Northern Aggression (as the Civil War was called when this author was but a wee lad in Virginia) blood brothers, fathers and sons, and Masonic Lodge brothers fought on opposing sides. Accounts of Southern and Yankee Masons putting aside their battlefield enmity to aid distressed worthy brother Masons or conduct funerals for fallen brothers from opposing latitudes have filled numerous books. Here are some stories with a different twist.

Beneath the bone-chilling cold water of Charleston Harbor, South Carolina, Lieutenant George E. Dixon maneuvered the Confederacy's newest secret weapon into attack position. The sandy-blonde Freemason was in command of the CSS *H.L. Hunley*, a primitive submarine that historically bore more of a resemblance to a steel-tubed coffin than to the nuclear submarines of the Cold War Era.

Lt. Dixon still carried a bullet in his upper thigh bone when he returned from the Battle of Shiloh to convalesce in Mobile, Alabama. It was there that he met Will Alexander, a fellow Freemason. As Dixon had been a steamboat engineer prior to the war, Bro. Alexander told him about the *Hunley* and solicited the young Lieutenant's help with the project.

The submarine was not only being built in Mobile, it also ran experimental trials in Mobile Bay. It was the need to break the Yankee blockade of Charleston Harbor that brought the strange craft to South Carolina on a flatbed railcar.

In Charleston, the *Hunley* proved its design as an instrument of death. Unfortunately for the South, it did not bring death to the enemy, but to her own Rebel crews. The first time she sank, five of her eight man crew drowned. These deaths were not even during the heat of battle, the *Hunley* sank while still moored at the wharf.

The second time she sank was in shallow waters within the harbor. All hands were killed, including her designer and namesake, Bro. Horace L. Hunley of Mt. Moriah Lodge #59 of New Orleans, Louisiana. Nevertheless, Dixon was confident that the *Hunley* could successfully sink an enemy ship, assuming the Atlantic weather provided a *very* tranquil sea. General Pierre Beauregard, a trained civil engineer, believed otherwise, but Dixon convinced the General to salvage the

submarine and give him a chance to prove its value.

Two weeks before commanding the submarine in combat, Dixon wrote a friend, "I am outside every night in a small boat so that there is not possible for any good night to pass without my being able to take advantage of it. I have my boat lying between Sullivan's and Long Islands and think that when the night does come that I will surprise the Yankees completely. The fleet offshore have drawings of the submarine and of course they have taken all precautions that it is possible for Yankee ingenuity to invent, but I hope to flank them yet."

On the night of February 17, 1864, Dixon and his seven volunteers set to sea with a one-hundred thirty-five pound "torpedo" strapped to the end of a one-hundred fifty foot spar projecting from the *Hunley's* bow. The craft looked something akin to a giant grey narwhal.

The crewmen sat in a row cranking a cam-shaft that turned the propeller. Dixon stood with his head in a viewing port as he controlled the dive planes and helm.

As the *Hunley* approached the enemy's 1,240 ton sloop, a steam powered man-of-war named the USS *Housatonic*, Yankee rifle shot bounced off the submarine's peering port. The Captain of the *Housatonic* fired both barrels of his shotgun, and an Ensign emptied his revolver at "the infernal submarine machine". Ignoring the ricocheting lead, Dixon steered true and rammed the Yankee warship in its starboard beam, just aft of the mizzenmast. He detached the torpedo and reversed course. As the *Hunley* pulled away from the *Housatonic*, a detonation line played out until it tripped a blasting cap. The resulting explosion set the sloop-of-war aflame, sinking her in three minutes. Newspapers reported that the Union Navy believed the craft had used an "underwater canon" to sink the *Housatonic*.

The *Hunley* surfaced briefly for Dixon to signal success to lookouts on Sullivan's Island, before slipping beneath the sea, where she lay undiscovered until 1995. When she was raised in 2000, the remains of eight men were recovered. Lt. Dixon and three of the crewmen were identified.

Unlike the February cold of 1864, when the *Hunley* was lost, April 17, 2004, was a warm Southern day in Charleston as Masons and Confederate re-enactors congregated for the funeral procession of Master Mason and Royal Arch Mason, Bro. Dixon, and his crew.

The entire officer line of both the Grand Lodge of South Carolina and the Grand Lodge of Alabama were in attendance with visiting Masons, all dressed in white Masonic aprons. It took one-hundred and forty years, but acacia sprigs were finally placed on Bro. Dixon's coffin as a bugler sounded Taps.

The life of Abraham Lincoln was taken by a noted Shakespearean actor. By coincidence, the life of Lincoln's eldest son was saved by another noted Shakespearean actor. The happenstance involving the President's son occurred in the late winter of 1864. Robert Todd Lincoln wrote of the event to Richard Watson Gilder, the editor of *The Century Magazine*. They published his letter in 1909:

"The incident occurred while a group of passengers were late at night purchasing their sleeping car places from the conductor who stood on the station platform at the entrance of the car. The platform was about the height of the car floor, and there was of course a narrow space between the platform and the car body. There was some crowding, and I happened to be pressed by it against the car body while waiting my turn. In this situation the train began to move, and by the motion I was twisted off my feet, and had dropped somewhat, with feet downward, into the open space, and was personally helpless, when my coat collar was vigorously seized and I was quickly pulled up and out to a secure footing on the platform. Upon turning to thank my rescuer I saw it was Edwin Booth, whose face was of course well known to me, and I expressed my gratitude to him, and in doing so, called him by name."

Edwin Thomas Booth, a noted Northern sympathizer was a member of New York Lodge #330 of New York City, New York. Edwin was the elder brother of Presidential assassin John Wilkes Booth.

John was not a Freemason, but belonged to a non-Masonic group called the Knights of the Golden Circle. Although it has been alleged that the KGC was influenced by Masonic author Albert Pike, it was actually Gen. George W. L. Bickley who founded and promoted the group. The KGC advocated the creation of a Southern Empire promoting slavery of non-whites, including the forcible annexation of Cuba, Mexico, and Central America as additional slave states.

General Pierre Gustave Toutant Beauregard of the Confederate States Army was offered a command in Brazil after the war, but the size of the command and rank offered were less than what he deemed acceptable for a man of his stature. Instead, he turned his attention to operating the Louisiana State Lottery and became quite wealthy. Beauregard was a Master Mason and a Knight Templar.

Other Southern soldiers settled throughout Brazil after the war. With Beauregard declining the offer of Emperor Dom Pedro II, Colonel William Hutchinson Norris became the most prominent Mason to move south of the South. Prior to the war, Norris was a United States Senator from Alabama and had been Grand Master of the Yellowhammer State.

The move to Brazil was logical and attractive for Confederate Masons. The country was a supporter of both the Confederacy and Freemasonry. The Emperor was a Freemason and his father had been a Grand Master. Norris founded *Vila dos Americanos* in São Paulo, Brazil. Today the city, better known by its English name of Americana, has a population of approximately 210,000. Beside the Square and Compass found on area tombstones, there are large Square and Compass sculptures exhibited throughout the city.

The Panama Pacific Line launched the 613 passenger ship SS *Virginia* in 1928. In 1937, the US Maritime Commission bought her and renamed the vessel the SS *Brazil,* pursuant to President Roosevelt's plan that she operate as a "Good Neighbor Ship" to that South American country.

On February 23, 1950, a retired Rear Admiral of the US Navy and his wife boarded the SS *Brazil* with the intention of immigrating to the country of the same name. The Admiral's name was Augustin T. Beauregard, the grand-nephew of General Pierre Beauregard.

April 17, 1865, Worshipful Master John Nichols opened a late afternoon meeting in Hiram Masonic Lodge #40 of Raleigh, North Carolina.

The city was already under martial law, when General Sherman received word that President Lincoln had been assassinated two days before. Fearing massive rioting, Sherman immediately issued orders for General Cox to strengthen the garrison and post additional sentries and pickets around Raleigh.

According to Hiram Lodge's history, the April meeting in the second floor Lodge Room was a mix of local Masons and Union officers who were Masons. "Suddenly, we heard the hasty footsteps of someone ascending the stairs to the hall, and the low clanking of the sword of an officer. Capt. W. C. Whitten of the Ninth Maine Regiment had come to apprise the group of what had happened, to order the officers to rejoin their respective commands and to advise the local men to hurry to their homes to protect their families."

Under these exigent circumstances, the men rushed out of the room, including Worshipful Master John Nichols, who failed to take time to properly close the lodge.

His oversight was officially corrected on April 17, 1915. With the much older Past Master Nichols still presiding, and other men appointed *pro tempore* to fill in for the departed Lodge officers, the meeting of April 17, 1865, was called to order and closed in due form, fifty years after opening.

CHAPTER 16

ONE DAY OF WONDER

A minority of jurisdictions still permit the Grand Masters of their states to make a man a "Mason at Sight". It is a seldom used machine that has always been fraught with controversy within the Fraternity.

Being made a "Mason at Sight" is different from conferring all three degree rituals on a candidate in a single day. The ancient Mason at Sight procedure was for the Grand Master to administer the Master Mason's obligation to the candidate, present him with an apron and trowel, and pronounce him a Mason. The handful of famous men who have been "made Masons at Sight" include President William Howard Taft, General Douglas MacArthur, and General George Marshall.

The example of President Taft represents the imprecise nature of the term "Mason at Sight". The Grand Master of Ohio, Charles S. Hoskinson, was present in Kilwinning Lodge #356 of Cincinnati on February 18, 1909. During the afternoon, Taft was obligated in both the First and Second degrees and received the lectures for those two degrees. In the evening, the Lodge conferred the entire Third Degree ritual. Because Taft was obligated in all three degrees and received the lectures in all three degrees, it would appear that this was a one day conferral instead of a Mason at Sight conferral. But an element of a one day conferral was missing.

Taft wasn't voted on as a member of Kilwinning Lodge until two months later, on April 14, 1909.

Benjamin Daniel Hyam was the third Grand Master of the State of California, but the first to face removal from office.

During the Mexican-American War, Hyam joined up as a way to get to the West Coast. He was present during the siege of Vera Cruz in March of 1847. He spent seventeen days of the siege in the Quartermasters Corps distributing supplies. While in Vera Cruz, he went through his degrees at Quitman Lodge #96. By the time October rolled around, he was anxious to head northward. He ended up in San Francisco, where he took up the trade of lawyer in the Jewish area of the community.

He was instrumental in establishing the Grand Lodge of California, and in May of 1852 was elected the state's third Grand Master. By August of that year, multiple charges of "Unmasonic Conduct" had been leveled against him.

The Grand Lodge convened on August 17, 1852, in San Francisco to address these charges. Grand Master Hyam was not present, as he had conveniently absented himself from the Golden State.

It was alleged that Hyam had charged $100 to make men "Masons at Sight" without their going through the Masonic ritual. One man had previously been rejected for membership in California Lodge #1 and another rejected in Shade Lodge #18. Additionally, Hyam was charged with interfering with a Worshipful Master while visiting a working Lodge, and had refused to obey the Master's gavel when "Called to Order".

Hyam contended that nothing in the State's Masonic Constitution or Lodge by-laws prevented his actions. He alleged that the charges were brought against him because of his religion and politics. A Grand Lodge Committee regretfully found that Hyam was correct, as to the law, not the prejudice. They ruled, "Of his possessing the power to do this, we have no doubt whatsoever." They also found, "Our present Grand Master has shamefully abused the powers of his office... employed that office for unworthy purposes...and made merchandise of Masonry by manufacturing Masons wholesale, even without being obliged to work the degrees."

In 1855, California adopted a code that prohibited the Grand Master from making Masons at Sight.

That California prohibition of 1855 came into play over a century later.

In February 1984, a gentleman petitioned Gothic Lodge #270 of Hamilton Square, New Jersey, for membership. Little did he know the trans-continental feud his petition would spark between two competing Grand Lodges.

Amos Alphonsus Muzyad Yakhoob was born in 1912 in Deerfield, Michigan, to Maronite Eastern Catholic immigrants from Lebanon. We know Amos better as the popular nightclub comedian, movie actor, television star, and founder of St. Jude Children's Research Hospital, Danny Thomas.

On March 15, 1984, Mr. Thomas finished a performance in Manhattan before traveling to Hamilton Square, where the Worshipful Master Daniel Wilson and Lodge officers conferred all three obligations on Bro. Thomas that evening.

When the Grand Master of California received word of what had occurred, he withdrew recognition of all New Jersey Lodges effective the twenty-ninth of August, and the Grand Lodge of California ratified his action.

New Jersey is one of the thirty-five states that have permitted one-day conferrals of all three degrees. California was one of the sixteen states that expressly prohibited such conferrals. An additional jurisdictional problem was that Mr. Thomas had his principal residence in Beverly Hills, California.

California decreed that all California Masons and Lodges were "to have no fraternal relations with a Mason carrying a New Jersey dues card ... including Scottish Rite, York Rite, Eastern Star and Order of Amaranth."

New Jersey claimed that Mr. Thomas was "a Citizen of the World" and refused to recognize California's claim under the "Doctrine of Exclusive Territorial Jurisdiction" between Grand Lodges.

California was unwilling to accept Mr. Thomas's application for dual membership, saying he would need to take all three degrees again in proper form.

By the nineteenth of October, the two Grand Lodges had worked out their chest bumping differences, and Bro. Thomas received dual memberships. The next year he received his Scottish Rite Masonry degrees in California and was active with Al Malaikah Shrine and their Children's Hospital in Los Angeles.

In one of his many speeches, Thomas answered the question as to why he had become a Mason:

"Because Masons care for those who cannot care for themselves. The Shriners have always been a favorite of mine because of their work for crippled and burned children. ... Masons are people of goodwill who want to "keep our kids alive" and we are doing this throughout the world. Our purpose is noble and humanitarian. Our labors will be crowned with success, for as Freemasons we will bring to our mission the best we have, regardless of what it demands from us in the way of sacrifice and service."

CHAPTER 17

DISTURB NOT THE SLEEP OF DEATH

Masonic rituals involving mortality, burial, and graves have stirred the public's fascination with cemeteries, tombstones, and haunted buildings associated with Freemasonry. This fascination borders on the bizarre when the Masonic tomb in question is a haunted several-hundred ton pyramid.

Frederick Adolphus Dorn was the Master of King David's Lodge #209 of San Luis Obispo, California, in 1891 and 1892. Dorn was from San Francisco, but moved to San Luis Obispo to practice law and was elected District Attorney. His wife, Cora B. Russell, was from a prominent local family.

Tragedy struck the Dorn family in May 1905. Fred Jr. was born and died on the twenty-third of May. His mother followed him three days later.

Heartbroken, Dorn purchased property in the San Luis Cemetery on a high knoll that had a strong supporting base of olive-green serpentine rock. Time has proven that it could support his proposed structure's massive weight. Since 1965, serpentine has been the Official State Rock of California.

Stonemasons hand hewed granite blocks for the imposing twenty-seven foot tall pyramid. The stones were quarried near Porterville, California, and transported one-hundred eighty miles to the cemetery on specially designed wagons. The mausoleum cost over $75,000 by the time it was completed in 1906. This was at a time when a typical five-room house could be purchased for $1,250. Carved within the stone are three names, along with their dates of birth and death: Cora Russel Dorn, Fred Adolphus Dorn Jr, and Fred Adolphus Dorn. Space was left to enter the father's date of death at a time when he would join his wife and child behind the copper door of the tomb, and the final three stones would be cemented into place. But, that day never came.

While on a luxury cruise to Australia in 1908, Dorn was smitten by New Zealand born Zoe Grey Wilkin and remarried. He returned to San Francisco, had three children with Zoe, and upon his death, was buried in Cypress Lawn Cemetery, San Francisco.

As of 2011, the Dorn Pyramid stands unsealed, looking out over a drive-in movie theater parking area. The copper door has turned green with a weathered patina. Three remaining blocks awaiting placement lay strewn on the ground in front of the door. In addition to a Masonic Square and Compass tooled into the pyramid's foundation, there is a message carved at the entrance to the tomb: "DISTURB NOT THE SLEEP OF DEATH". These eerie words have gone unheeded by Halloween revelers. A local legend tells of celebrants knocking on the tomb's copper door twelve times at midnight and receiving an immediate spine tingling thirteenth answering knock from within. In some years, private security guards have been stationed at the tomb.

The six-story Knox Building in Enid, Oklahoma, was the largest and most active Masonic Temple in the region when it was completed in 1924. Besides the Lodge Rooms on the uppermost two floors, the Temple included a concert hall, a community theater, a banquet hall, and numerous rental areas.

The top two levels of the Lodge were hastily and unceremoniously sealed in 1946 and remained so until 1981. Adding to the mystery of the sealed Temple, no one was permitted onto these two floors, and the owners refused to sell the building, ignoring several quite lucrative offers.

In spite of speculations of foul play and Masonic cover-ups, no ghostly sounds are associated with the building. However, the building does have "The Lights" as patrons to the local cafes call them.

The mysterious lights attributed to the ghost of an elevator repairman can be seen flickering in the unoccupied upper floors. Even the highly respected director of the Enid Symphony has reported a ghostly stairway encounter with "George", the repairman's ghost. At least he isn't named Otis.

Rockton Masonic Lodge #316 is on the National Register of Historic Places. It should also be on the National Register of Haunted Places. The Lodge was originally constructed in Kent, Ohio, as a 7,335 square foot family residence.

"The Homestead", as it was called, was the Italianate-styled home of Marvin Kent. It took four years to complete, from 1880 to 1884. Marvin was the influential industrialist and banker who brought the Atlantic and Great Western Railroad to Franklin Mills. In recognition of his commercial impact for the community, the city changed its name to Kent

Four presidents were guests of the Kents in their mansion with its spacious grand ballroom: Warren Harding,

William Howard Taft, William McKinley, and Benjamin Harrison. These presidents were probably kept warm by the home's twenty fireplaces.

Marvin's son, William, married Miss Kittie North in 1874. In 1896, she was tragically burned alive on the third floor of the mansion, when a kerosene lamp exploded.

The Rockton Masonic Lodge acquired the building in 1923. Since then, the Tiler has had one eavesdropper who has repeatedly caused him problems. Kittie's ghost reportedly would scratch items that could reflect her burned image, such as mirrors and polished surfaces. Unable to cry out, she would disrupt meetings and scare guests with banging noises.

Kittie isn't the only ghost associated with the Kents. Nellie Dingley was the first librarian when the Kent Free Library was built near the site of the Masonic Lodge on land donated by Marvin Kent. She died of pneumonia in 1918, during World War One, while volunteering as a Red Cross nurse in France.

Her apparition has been sighted wandering the library halls in a period nurse's uniform, probably looking for a good book of Masonic Trivia, Amusements & Curiosities.

Bro. William Brockmeier of Mt. Moriah Masonic Lodge #40 in St. Louis, Missouri, conducted over 5,586 Masonic funeral services. The exact number is unknown because Brockmeier didn't maintain records until 1911. By that time, he'd already conducted many services.

One may wonder how he found the time to hold a fulltime job and officiate at so many services. The answer lies in the nature of his "usual vocation". He was employed as a Stationary Engineer with the American Brake Company and worked the night shift his entire life. This allowed him to be free during the daytime to conduct services for the forty-eight lodges in the greater St. Louis area.

Archived trestleboards from the St. Louis area attest to the "dignity and eloquence" of his presentations. His commitment to the craft and his brother Masons was remarkable when the amount of time involved in contacting the families, obtaining the brothers' Masonic records, and attending fifty-six hundred services without remuneration is calculated.

Bro. Brockmeier's own Masonic funeral was "well attended" on May 29, 1947. He was eighty-one years of age and a true Master of the Craft.

Is the Annapolis Stone evidence of the first practice of Freemasonry in North America? The engraved stone has the appearance of a gravestone laid for a brother in Acadia or what in modern times we call Nova Scotia in the Annapolis Basin of Goat Island.

While at Harvard in 1827, Dr. Charles Thomas Jackson, M.D. (a brother-in-law to Ralph Waldo Emerson) of Boston, Massachusetts, went on a geological exploration of Nova Scotia with his friend Francis Alger. Twenty-nine years later, he wrote a letter to J.W. Thornton detailing the stone's discovery:

June 2, 1856
Dear Sir:
> *When Francis Alger and myself made a mineralogical survey of Nova Scotia in 1827, we discovered upon the shore of Goat Island, in Annapolis Basin, a gravestone partly covered with sand and lying on the shore. It bore the Masonic emblems, square and compass, and had the figures 1606 cut on it.*
> *The rock was a flat slab of trap rock, common in the vicinity. At the ferry from Annapolis to Granville we saw a large rounded rock with this inscription "La Belle*

1649." These inscriptions were undoubtedly intended to commemorate the place of burial of French soldiers who came to Nova Scotia, "Annapolis Royal, I'Acadie," in 1603.

Coins, buttons and other articles originally belonging to these early French settlers, are found in the soil of Goat Island in Annapolis Basin.

The slab, bearing date 1606, I had it brought over by the ferryman to Annapolis, and ordered it to be packed in a box to be sent to the Old Colony Pilgrim Society (of Plymouth, Mass.), but Judge Haliburton, then Thomas Haliburton, Esq., prevailed on me to abandon it to him, and he now has it carefully preserved. On a late visit to Nova Scotia I found that the Judge had forgotten how he came by it, and so I told him all about it.

Yours truly,

C. T. Jackson

In 1876, the Royal Canadian Institute was having its new building constructed. The Trustees instructed Dr. Charles Scadding to have the stone mounted into the wall of the new building.

The intent was that the stone's inscription would be left exposed for visitors to read. This intent was not conveyed to the workmen, and the irreplaceable stone was literally embedded within the two-foot thick walls. A reward of $1000 was offered to discover the location of the stone within the walls and recover it. No one has ever claimed the reward.

As to the stone's Masonic provenance, the two-foot long stone was clearly marked with a Square and Compass and bore a legible date of 1606. That was 111 years before the formation of the Grand Lodge in England. For this reason, anti-Masonic historians promote the theory that it was the tombstone for an operative carpenter, because carpenters also used a square and compass in their woodwork.

Like the Mystery Pit on Oak Island of Nova Scotia that many claim is the hiding place for ethereal Knights Templar gold, we may never know.

Continuing on the topic of pre-Grand Lodge graves, there is the equally strange case of John Cowane. Brother Cowane sat as a member of Parliament representing Stirling, Scotland, from 1625 until his sudden death in 1633. His death was so unexpected, that he died "intestate" (without a will). Always noted for his public mindedness and philanthropy, his younger brother honored Cowane's wishes that 40,000 merks (each silver merk was worth two-thirds of a Scottish Pound) be donated to build a hospital and almshouse for the needy of the burgh.

Cowane's massive tombstone bears a simple crest and the centerpiece of a prominent numeral "4". Two Master Mason symbols of a Square and Compass act as decorative serifs at the ends of the two arms of the "4".

When the first Grand Lodge of England was formed in 1717, there were only two degrees. The third degree was not reported until 1725. The Fourth Degree of Mark Master came even later as an honorary degree for Fellow Crafts. So, why was the seldom seen symbol of a Masonic Four chiseled into this wealthy merchant's tombstone a century before historians believe it had meaning?

In a May 2009 interview, rock drummer Bryan Mantia discussed his six years working on the "Guns N' Roses" album *Chinese Democracy*. When discussing the multi-storied building where they were to record, he related, "The studio didn't have the right vibe. So, he (Jeff Greenberg) tells me there's a haunted Masonic temple upstairs where the Masons would give their speeches, and nobody ever goes up there. It was a like an abandoned theater. So we go up, he opens the door, and I'm thinking, *We've got to set up here* (original emphasis). We found the sweet spot and I set up the drums there...and that's where the drums stayed for six years."

Between 1822 and 1854, a plot of land in Richmond, Texas, named for Bro. William Morton went by the simple handle of Morton Cemetery. From 1855 to 1890, it was known as the Michael DeChaumes Cemetery. From 1890 until 1940, Morton Masonic Lodge #72 operated it as the Richmond Masonic Cemetery. In 1940, the Lodge turned it over to the Morton Cemetery Association, and the name reverted back to the original Morton Cemetery.

The only problem with the name is the fact that Bro. William Morton isn't buried in the Masonic cemetery that bears his name.

Morton was one of the "Old Three Hundred" settlers of 1822 who obtained Mexican land grants in Stephen F. Austin's Texas colony. Morton received 1 ½ leagues of land on one side of the Brazos river and "a labor" (177 acres) on the other bank.

One of Morton's brother Masons by the name of Robert Gillespie (or Gelaspie) met the grim reaper as the result of foul play. Bro. Morton set aside land for a cemetery and buried the brother beneath a handmade brick tomb. The tomb still stands as the first known Masonic landmark in Texas.

Why isn't William Morton buried in his own cemetery? In 1833, Morton was caught in and swept away by the famous Brazos Flood. His body was never recovered.

Davenport, Iowa, was the home to Davenport Lodge #37, a four-story building on the corner of Brady Street and 7th Street. When the building was dedicated in 1923, many of the Lodge's four-hundred brethren were law enforcement officers and detectives.

In 1996, the building was sold to Palmer College and renamed Lyceum Hall & Museum.

Legend, rumor, and tall tales say the spirits of early Blue Lodge Masons, who wore policemen's blue, refused to leave and caused much mischief with knocking, the calling of commands to "Halt!", and the blowing of whistles. Perhaps they are waiting for someone to bring donuts?

In 1979, the Canadian National Public Broadcasters aired a segment about the haunting of a Mother Tucker's Restaurant. It seems that Mother Tucker purchased the old Masonic Temple in Winnipeg, and the departed Lodge brethren were not happy in their new "digs".

The Masonic ghosts purportedly turned over salt and pepper shakers, moaned, and their apparitions made startling appearances. One ghost was described by a witness as wearing "a top hat and eighteenth century black tails".

The restaurant had even tried to bust these ghosts by removing the "well used, but empty coffin" the new owners found stored in the abandoned Masonic attic, but to no avail.

The beautiful Masonic Temple at the corner of Kinau and Makiki Streets in Hawaii is reportedly haunted. The building was part of the residence of Princess Kekaulike, sister of Queen Kapiolani. Later, it was a maternity home. Instead of checking out hotel sponsored synthetic luaus and plastic tourist attractions when in Hawaii, brothers should visit the Temple to discover the true *spirit* of the islands.

The Albert Pike Memorial Masonic Temple in North Little Rock, Arkansas, is reportedly haunted by the ghostly specter of Confederate General Albert Pike. A prolific author of

Masonic works, Pike is well known to all students of Masonic history, rituals, morals, and dogma.

Unfortunately, not all Masonic brothers leave our temporal soil on good terms with their jurisdiction's Grand Lodge. Rosehill Cemetery in Chicago is "home" to some strange brothers and a strange monument.

The Lincoln Park Masonic Lodge built a Masonic monument in Rosehill bearing an enormous sphere that would dwarf the Lodge pillars of Boaz or Jachin. This globe has a bizarre trait; it falls off about once every decade.

Many residents (those living nearby, not those in the cemetery) believe it is because the Lodge's Charter was revoked by the Grand Lodge of Joliet, when members were discovered experimenting with "black arts".

Is it possible the banished Lincoln Park members are disturbed or trying to get revenge? Perhaps this will never be answered, like the other eternal question, "Why do cats always cuddle up to visitors who are allergic to cats and ignore those who aren't?"

A historical account dated 1847 relates that a Jew by the name of Benjamin Levy had become friends with an "English Clergyman of the Baptist denomination" on the island of St. Thomas in the Virgin Islands. Both the Baptists and the Spanish Roman Catholics had a missionary presence on the island.

The Baptist clergyman contracted a "Tropical Illness" and was nearing death when he summoned his friend. The preacher asked the Jew to provide a burial service and read resurrection scripture the preacher had marked in his Bible when the time came. Levy suggested that it would be inappropriate, if not hypocritical, and that he could not in good conscience read these passages on such a solemn time.

The Baptist clergyman, knowing the Jew was a brother Freemason, asked him, "to say the prayers customary to our fraternity", apparently preferring the services of a non-trinitarian brother to that of a Spanish Priest.

The service was attended by Masonic brothers and Baptists from St. Thomas, Puerto Rico, and Jacmel, Haiti. No mention was made if the Spanish Priest was present.

Both American and French flags fly over his grave. He has been honored on US Postage stamps in 1952, 1957, and 1977. In 1900, he was honored on a US Commemorative Silver Dollar. Who is this Freemason brother?

He is Marie-Joseph Paul Yves Roch Gilbert du Motier, Marquis de La Fayette. Americans spelled his name, Lafayette, and he was instrumental in helping the American colonies defeat the British. George Washington personally cited his friend and Masonic brother for "bravery and military ardour" at the Battle of Brandywine in September 1777.

On Lafayette's trip to America in 1824 and 1825, he attended the Grand Lodge of Delaware and was made an Honorary Member, the Grand Lodge of Maine, the Grand Lodge of New Jersey, the Grand Lodge of Maryland, the Grand Lodge of South Carolina, the Grand Lodge of Illinois, the Grand Lodge of Louisiana, and received another Honorary membership in the Grand Lodge of Tennessee.

When he returned to France in 1825, Bro. Lafayette took with him 2,400 pounds of soil dug from the battle sites on which he fought for the colonies. The soil was used in his grave when he died in 1834, as well as, a shovel of soil from George Washington's grave at Mount Vernon. He shares the grave with his wife in the Cemetery of Picpus. Their grave is near a mass grave that includes her family and a hundred other nobles beheaded during the French Revolution.

By all accounts, Bro. Thomas Amner of Santa Cruz Lodge #38 of California was a robust young man, when he was accidentally shot and killed in 1885. The Lodge mourned the loss of the Adonis-like young man and made suitable arrangements for his Masonic burial and the stationing of full-time watchmen at his graveside for a period of two weeks.

Graveside watchmen are not part of Masonic tradition or practice, so what prompted the brethren of Santa Cruz Lodge to take this extraordinary step and expense?

Nearby medical schools were in need of cadavers, and there had been a spate of recent cases where resurrectionists (body snatchers) had dug up youthful cadavers to sell to the schools. The Lodge believed that their young brother's body would no longer be prime fare for the lurking grave robbers after spending two weeks in the ground.

The July 18, 1954, edition of *The Tampa Tribune* reported that "An iron coffin bearing a Masonic emblem, a skeleton believed to be that of Ferdinand DeSoto, the Spanish explorer, is owned by Crescent Lodge No. 133 of Arkansas City (Kansas). The casket was found on a farm near Ferguson, Arkansas, weighs 300 pounds, is five feet in length, and elaborately engraved. It contains a skeleton, a sword, bits of armor, and several coins."

There is a problem. Almond Dunbar Fisk received US Patent #5920 for the first cast-iron casket in America in November of 1848, three hundred years after DeSoto died in 1542.

Anyone who has taken US Civics in high school knows that in the Virginia House of Burgesses on March 23, 1775, the great American patriot Patrick Henry said, "Give me liberty, or give me death!"   Well, not really, it never happened.

In 1817, the new United States Attorney General by the name of William Wirt published a book called the *Life and Character of Patrick Henry*. The book contained that never before heard fanciful quote. The Virginia Statesman and friend of Patrick Henry, John Taylor, called the book, "a splendid novel." Wirt's imposturous book was unequivocally more historical fiction, than biographical truth.

Skip forward to Christmas of 2003 in Washington, D.C. when Bill Fecke, manager of the Congressional Cemetery, received a mysterious phone call, *"What do you know about William Wirt's skull?"*

What Fecke knew was that Wirt had been entombed in 1834, with both body and skull intact. When the mysterious person next called, the voice asked, *"What do you know about a grave robbery in your cemetery eighteen years ago?"* At this point, Fecke went to check the tomb and discovered that the door's lock had been forcibly broken and was rusted. A heavy granite slab had been propped to conceal the small door.

Fecke's next call was from City Councilman Jim Graham, *"Are you missing William Wirt's head?"* It appeared that someone had anonymously delivered a rusted red metal box containing a skull to the Councilman. Painted on the box in block letters of old gold paint were the words, "Hon. Wm. Wirt"

The situation inside the tomb need to be checked, and the Cemetery District obtained permission to enter the tomb. What they found were chaotically strewn remains. As months passed without any determination of the bones in the tomb or the skull in the box, it was inevitable that newspapers would get ahold of the story, and they did.

At this point the origins of the skull became less anonymous. Councilman Graham said he'd gotten the box from Allan Stypeck, a dealer in used books. Stypeck said he'd obtained the box from the estate of Robert L. White. At the time of his death, White had a collection of forty plus skulls and a dozen shrunken heads. Graham and Stypeck both denied being the mysterious original caller.

Anthropologists from the Smithsonian Institute examined the remains of the fifteen people who belonged in the tomb. They determined that Wirt's coffin was indeed missing a skull and the connecting vertebrae. As the floor was swept and examined for the vertebrae, a sixteenth set of bones was discovered. These belonged to an unknown newborn girl, and were hidden beneath a ladder leading down into the tomb's cryptic chamber.

William Wirt was a noted trial lawyer. In 1807, President Jefferson requested that he prosecute former Vice-President Aaron Burr in his trial for treason. Wirt's eloquent closing argument is still studied by aspiring neophyte trial lawyers.

What makes Wirt interesting to Masons is that he was *the only candidate ever nominated for the United States presidency by the Anti-Masonic Party*. Wirt's presidential bid began at the national convention for the Anti-Masonic Party in 1832. He won the nomination in spite of the startling fact that ***Wirt was a Freemason and gave a speech at the convention defending Freemasonry!***

Documents from the period show the Anti-Masonic party was more focused against Andrew Jackson's liberal democratic principles associated with Freemasonry, than against the fraternity itself.

In the national election, Wirt only carried the single state of Vermont. Within four years of the election, the Anti-Masonic party was on its last legs. The Masonic fraternity, which had suffered temporarily devastating loses, was experiencing phenomenal national growth in membership.

Wirt's skull was reunited with his other remains in 2005, and the tomb was resealed. The identity of the baby girl is still a mystery.

CHAPTER 18

NOT ALL QUALIFY

In California, saloon keepers and bar keepers were disqualified from becoming Freemasons.

Connecticut Masons disqualified any "Stupid Atheist" or Libertine from membership.

Arizona disqualified "Eunuchs and Illiterates". In all fairness, Arkansas, California, Connecticut, Minnesota, New York, and South Dakota also disqualified eunuchs in 1917. Georgia and Wisconsin disqualified them without using the snippy word. They simply required candidates to have their "Entire Organs" and be "Unmutilated".

Sumo wrestlers would have a problem in 1917 Florida where candidates were deemed disqualified for health reasons, if they were not "their due weight".

Quasimodo had better stick to bell-ringing if he lived in Georgia. They disqualified hunchbacks, but in West Virginia, they were eligible. Illegitimacy of birth did not disqualify in Georgia, but it did in Virginia.

South Dakota had a prejudice against any man with a "Cork Leg". Apparently South Dakotans had more of a problem with pirates than Masons did in Missouri, for cork legs did not disqualify applicants in the "Show Me" state.

Although not explicitly stated, politicians in New York might have a problem being elected to a local Masonic Lodge. The State's Grand Lodge disqualified "Scandalous men" and Fools.

Wyoming turned a blind eye to any man with a "Glass Eye". They likewise disqualified a man for shooting himself in the hip with the loaded revolver carried in his pocket while riding on horseback (you would have thought that being a fool would have sufficed).

Bro. Mordecai Peter Centennial Brown was elected into the Baseball Hall of Fame, but was nearly rejected for Masonic membership.

Starting in 1906, the right-handed Chicago Cubs hurler won twenty or more games for six consecutive seasons. In 1908, he became the first professional pitcher to throw four consecutive shut-out games. Adding to his skill was the fact that he was a pretty good switch hitter. Brown was noted for his wobbling pitches that twisted and jerked the ball with baffling unpredictability on its trip to home plate. Fans chalked it up to Brown's skill. Opponents claimed it was the fact that he had lost two fingers in a coal mining accident, hence his nickname of "Three Fingered Brown".

When Brown petitioned for membership in Edward Dobbins Lodge #164 of Lawrenceville, Illinois, the matter of his missing digits was referred to the Grand Lodge. With Grand Lodge approval, the Cubs' ace received his degrees between March and July of 1925.

Prior to the Civil War, several Northern Grand Lodges (but not all) had constitutions, and numerous Lodges had bylaws, that forbid the acceptance of a man who possessed slaves or was engaged in slave trading.

Landmarks in Freemasonry are the ancient immutable prescripts of the Fraternity. Universal to all jurisdictions is the required belief in a Supreme Being, the immortality of the soul, and that a volume of sacred law is indispensable to a Lodge. The lists of landmarks vary by jurisdiction from six to twenty-two. In English and American Lodges, one of the ancient landmarks is that no woman can be a Mason.

This landmark is not universal to all of the 165 countries where Lodges exist. Lodges for women only Masons, as well as, coed Lodges, have existed for over a century.

There are approximately 15,400 Masonic Blue Lodges in the United States. Of these, only three are sororities for women Masons, all with Charters from the Grand Lodge of Belgium; one each in New York City, Washington, D.C., and Los Angeles. That is not to say the regular Lodges recognize these distaff members as Masons. Women's Lodges are considered clandestine in most jurisdictions.

The Order of Women Freemasons has nearly six thousand members in fifty countries. This compares to roughly thirty-four thousand Lodges and five and a half million male members worldwide.

Infants cannot join Masonic organizations, but the Grand Chapter of the Order of Eastern Star of Ohio appointed the six week old baby boy of their Grand Secretary the "Grand Chapter Baby" in September 1900. The infant's name was Otway E. Shearer. His monogram was the same as theirs, OES.

CHAPTER 19

UNCONVENTIONAL

Joel Roberts Poinsett was Deputy Grand Master of South Carolina and in line for the Grand Master's chair when President Martin Van Buren appointed him Secretary of War. His Masonic career included time as Worshipful Master of both Recovery Lodge #31 in Greenville, South Carolina, and Solomons Lodge #1 in Charleston. Poinsett had been a Congressman from South Carolina prior to receiving his appointment as Minister to Mexico in 1825. It wasn't until 1896 that the United States changed the title of Ministers to that of Ambassadors.

Poinsett's five years in Mexico were marked with much political controversy, as well as, Masonic controversy. He introduced York Rite Masonry to the politically liberal members of the Mexican government. This was in sharp contrast to the prevalent Scottish Rite Consistories or *Escosses* which were noted for their membership of the conservatives in the government.

Under Poinsett's guidance, the Grand Lodge of New York granted Charters to five liberal *Yorkino* Lodges. In 1830, Poinsett was recalled to Washington, but Freemasonry continued to flourish in our neighbor to the south.

In 1836, General Santa Anna, who styled himself as "The Napoleon of the West", lay siege to the Alamo for shy of a fortnight. Whether the General knew Davy Crockett was a Freemason, or not, when he ordered his execution is unknown. Santa Anna did give protection to Mrs. Suzanna Dickenson whose husband Almaron had told her to display his Masonic apron, in hopes of saving her life and that of their child. Santa Anna personally saw to her safety and the well-being of her child. He even offered to support the baby into adulthood, an offer the Widow Dickenson refused.

Upon his capture, Santa Anna's life was spared by Freemason James Sylvester when the General gave the Masonic "Grand Hailing Sign of Distress". The General also displayed that secret fraternal sign to Freemason Sam Houston.

One of Santa Anna's guards, John Stiles, claimed the General presented him with his Masonic apron. In an 1853 photograph, Santa Anna is dressed in a white Masonic "Lodge Apron". These linen aprons are made available to brethren attending meetings who have not brought their own apron with them. Many Mexican Military Lodges had their records destroyed or lost during the fighting of the 1800s, and there are no extant records of Santa Anna's Lodge affiliation.

Santa Anna was returned to Mexico and was in and out of favor as governments changed leaderships. In 1855, liberal forces overthrew the government, and Santa Anna fled to Cuba. By 1869, he was exiled in New York City. He brought with him a shipment of a rubbery substance called chicle. Santa Anna hoped the inexpensive and plentiful chicle could be mixed successfully with natural rubber, thus making him a wealthy man. It couldn't, and the penniless General died in 1876.

The man helping Santa Anna promote chicle was a glassblower and inventor by the name of Thomas Adams. After a year of failed experiments using chicle to make impractical umbrellas, boots, bicycle tires, and toys, Adams was ready to throw in the towel, or better yet, dump a warehouse full of chicle in the Atlantic.

By chance, he saw a girl chewing flavored paraffin wax, a precursor to modern chewing gum, and he came up with a scheme to redeem some of his expenses. Little did he realize that it would make him a fortune, create a new industry, and generate numberless books on the poor etiquette of gum chewing in public.

By 1871, Thomas had invented and patented a machine that produced his sarsaparilla flavored gum into thin sliced strips. In 1888, he hit the jackpot when he created a gum called Tutti-Frutti and became the first manufacturer in the world to sell gum from vending machines. He started with machines in the New York City subway stations before expanding to cafes and office buildings.

Having sunk our teeth into the Masonic connection to gum, let's go back to Dr. Poinsett. He was by trade a physician with a penchant for botany. He co-founded the National Institute for the Promotion of Science in 1842. It became part of the Smithsonian Institution twenty years later.

While in Mexico, he came across a winter blooming plant that was called *cuetlaxochiti* by the Aztecs. He collected and shipped numerous specimens back to his South Carolinian plantation. Even though the Mexican natives of Taxco claimed the plants had medicinal properties, Dr. Poinsett was unable to discover any. Nevertheless, he was impressed with the blooms and gave samples to his friends. These horticulturalist friends used his name as the eponym for the plant that we know today as the *Poinsettia*.

The plant remained a minor novelty until Paul Ecke took a commercial interest in the plant. Paul's father, Albert, had brought his son to California in 1900 while on his way from Germany to open a health spa in Fiji; the family never made it to the island nation. Albert operated a fruit orchard and dairy farm near Hollywood, California. His son Paul suggested they could grow poinsettias and possibly sell the unknown winter flower at Christmas time as a holiday novelty and decoration.

They started by selling them from Hollywood flower stands in 1911. In 1923, the Paul Ecke Ranch began shipping full "mother plants" to greenhouses as the demand for the seasonal flowers slowly increased. In 1960, a breakthrough came with the development of a variety that could be grown successfully in greenhouses from cuttings, and the tie between the poinsettia and the Christmas holiday season fully blossomed in the public's mind.

Paul Ecke was a fifty-year Golden Veteran of Oceanside-San Dieguito Lodge #381. His son, Paul Jr. was also a member of the same Lodge.

The first license for a commercial radio station was issued September 19, 1921, in Springfield, Massachusetts. Wireless transmission was in its infancy. The first broadcast of a baseball game had taken place the month before on August 5 for a game between the Pittsburg Pirates and the Philadelphia Phillies. It would be even later before stations developed news bureaus and regular broadcasts.

In between these events, the first wireless broadcast of a lecture on Freemasonry was delivered by John Whicher, the Grand Secretary of the State of California. It was transmitted on September 3, 1921, from a tower erected atop the Fairmont Hotel in San Francisco. The principal audience was Masons and their wives gathered in Woodbridge Lodge #131 around a radio receiver, two hundred miles away. Those few Masons who privately owned radio receivers were able to pick up the transmission as far away as Santa Barbara.

Grand Secretary John Whicher was noted for telling interesting anecdotal stories. Here are three that stand out. The first occurred in 1902, when he was the Worshipful Master of King David's Lodge #209.

"When I was Master of the Lodge at San Luis Obispo, we had an epidemic of blackballs. Someone continued to stop all who petitioned. I was satisfied that one of the employees of a corporation operating throughout the state was responsible for this unmasonic conduct. I was well acquainted with one of the employers for whom the offending brother worked. I fully discussed the situation with the employer, who happened to be a Mason, and I inquired if it would be possible for him to have the brother transferred to some other locality for a while. This was done and no more blackballs appeared in that Lodge."

At an annual communication of the Grand Lodge, officers of Forest Lodge #66 in Alleghany, California, approached the Grand Secretary with a problem: could the rules be changed about the Master wearing a silk top hat? The problem was that each year the new Master's head was a different size, thus requiring the purchase of a new expensive hat. Sometimes a brother sitting *Pro Tempore* in the East had a hat that didn't fit. Whicher told them to see him the next day before they returned home, and he would have a solution to their problem. That afternoon, Whicher purchased the largest silk hat he could locate, a 7 ¾ head size silk top hat. He presented it to the brethren of Forest Lodge along with a box of inch wide cloth lamp wicks, telling them to insert the wicks in the sweat band as needed to size the hat down to whoever was sitting in the Oriental Chair.

The third story involved the law. "One day when I was Grand Secretary, a policeman appeared at my office with a bedraggled man in tow. The policeman introduced himself, 'My name is Herlihy, a Sergeant of Police. I am not a Mason. I am an Irish-Catholic. This man is deaf and dumb. I picked him up for begging. He had this pin on his coat.' The Sergeant showed me a Square and Compass lapel pin, and continued, 'I knew you didn't want your brothers to be begging on the streets, so I brought him up to you.' I took the Sergeant's prisoner into the adjoining room and asked him what was his racket? If he was just foolish, and really in need, I would help him. But the man paid no matter to my questions and I returned him to the Sergeant saying, 'This man is not a Mason. He is a liar.' At which point, the man threw up his hands and said, "Oh hell, what's the use?' The Sergeant returned the next day to say the magistrate had sentenced the imposter to six months for falsely impersonating a Mason."

In Biblical references, Jewish lore, and Freemasonry allegory, the sprig of acacia is a symbol of the immortality of the soul. Moses constructed the Ark of the Covenant from the wood of the acacia (Exodus 25:10-22), and the Hebrews planted acacias at the head of graves.

The most famous modern acacia tree, known as the solitary tree or *L'Arbre du Ténéré*, was located in the Sahara desert region of Niger. The next nearest tree was one hundred and twenty miles away. So significant was the tree, that it was depicted on maps of the region. In 1973, this remote tree was struck and killed by a drunken Libyan truck driver. The dead tree was placed on display in the Niger National Museum. Where the *L'Arbre du Ténéré* once stood is a metal sculpture representation of an acacia tree.

Honey produced from the pollen of acacia trees has been called *The Immortal Honey*. The name is not derived from the acacia's symbolism in Freemasonry of an immortal soul, but from a unique property of the clear nectar. Unlike other honeys, acacia honey does not crystalize below 104 F . It also has thixotropic properties, viz, after sitting in a refrigerator, it solidifies into a jelly, but as soon as it is stirred or shaken, the jelly liquifies, and the acacia honey can be poured. All of the world's commercially produced acacia honey comes from Italy.

Of forty thousand species of spiders, all are believed to be carnivorous, except one. The *Bagheera kiplingi* is named in honor of Freemason Rudyard Kipling. This vegetarian spider survives on the nectar and protein rich beltian bodies or nubs on the leaves of the Central American trees where they live. The trees are acacias.

Have Freemasons always referred to the Supreme Being as The Great Architect of the Universe? No, it came into Masonry in 1723 from Christian theologians and preachers.

Saint Thomas Aquinas wrote in his 1265 *Summa Theologica*, "God, Who is the first principle of all things, may be compared to things created as the *architect* is to things designed (*ut artifex ad artificiata*)."

French theologian John Calvin, of the Protestant Reformation, repeatedly used the pseudonym "the Supreme Architect", "the Great Architect", and "the Architect of the Universe" when referring to the Deity. He likewise referred to nature as "the architecture of the Universe".

Puritan theologian Cotton Mather called God "the Divine Architect" in his writings of 1684.

These, and dozens more, were all before the formation of modern Speculative Freemasonry.

Reverend Doctor James Anderson was a Presbyterian minister who was a student of Calvin's teachings and Puritan writings. Anderson's *Constitution of 1723* was republished in the colonies by Benjamin Franklin in 1734, which gave it a wide distribution among Freemasons on both sides of the Atlantic.

In keeping with the Christian theologians who preceded him, Rev. Anderson referred to the Supreme Being as "The Great Architect of the Universe", and the name has been used in Freemasonry ever since.

Freemasons collect a wide variety of Masonic collectibles. Some are rather straightforward such as Masonic Pennies or Shekels from Lodges and Royal Arch Chapters. Some are traditional like postage stamps of the world and First

Day Cachet Covers. Some are academic like biographies of famous men who were Masons. Some collect bookplates. Yes, they are paper plates, but not the kind that go into the microwave oven.

What are bookplates? They are small labels glued to the inside of the front cover of a book to indicate ownership. Most are rectangular, but they may be cut to shape a theme, such as a shield or an animal or an open book. Another name for bookplates is *Ex Libris* foils.

Book owners today use "Stick-on" labels generated on a computer printer, rubber-stamp images, or those unsolicited address labels that come in the mail seeking donations. But there was a time when books had leather covers, and any quality home library had books with the owner's custom bookplates affixed therein.

Before the invention of bookplates, owners marked their valuable tomes with book rhymes that threatened harm or warning to any would be thief. *"Thief, thief, go away; Steal this book not today; it belongs to lawyer Thomas Jay."* or *"May the fleas of a thousand camels infest the armpits of any who dare steal this book from Jacob Samuels"*

When bookplates became popular as testimony of ownership, some carried on the tradition of a warning rhyme, a coat-of-arms, or a family motto. Others bore a motif reflecting the owner's distinctive tastes. They can be elaborately commissioned engravings like the ones designed by Paul Revere or a generic text only label, "Property of John Smith".

The earliest known book about Masonic bookplates was *Masonic Book-Plates* by Robert Day of London and was printed 1904. This was followed by *Remarks on some Masonic Book-Plates in America and their Owners* by Alexander Winthrop Pope of Boston. Pope's work was in two parts. Part One was published in 1908. Part Two was published in 1911. More material followed in 1918, when *Masonic Bookplates* by Winward Prescott of Boston was printed by The Society of Bookplate Bibliophiles.

So, next time you open an old book on Masonry, check the inside cover. It might have belonged to a famous Mason or even have a Paul Revere bookplate bearing his armorial seal of the Lodge of St. Andrew with Paul's autograph. They do exist.

Freemasons operating under dire straits and far away from their home Lodges have made due with whatever was available to hold a brotherly communication.

Two Lodges are known to have fashioned officers' jewels from empty food tins during the California Gold Rush: Benicia Lodge #5 of Benicia, California, in 1850; and Pacific Lodge of Butte County, California, in 1850. A third Lodge, Lawrence Lodge # 6 of Lawrence, Kansas, is known to have likewise made use of empty food tins in 1855.

When the Masons of St. Louis, California, received a dispensation in 1856 to open St. Louis Masonic Lodge #86, a local blacksmith came to their aid by fashioning Lodge Jewels from a punctured kerosene drum.

Allied Australian prisoners of war fashioned officers' jewels out of empty chocolate tins, while held by the Japanese in the infamous Changi Prison of Singapore during World War Two. Their ballot box was "jerry rigged" from a cork float and a steel canteen.

CHAPTER 20

PRESIDENTS AND SUCH

The last time that President Warren Gamaliel Harding signed his name was to inscribe his signature in the Lodge Bible of Lafayette Lodge #241 of Seattle, Washington.

Bro. Harding's ship had berthed in Seattle on his return trip from Alaska in 1923.

The voyage had not gone well. The President had contracted ptomaine poisoning while dining on crabs aboard his Army transport, the USS *Henderson*. Radar did not yet exist, and the *Henderson* rammed one of her escorting destroyers in Seattle's thick "marine layer" fog.

To make matters worse, Harding caught a cold while giving a speech in the University of Washington's Stadium. Instead of crawling into a warm bed, the President followed the speech by riding in an open-car parade and finished the evening by conducting an outdoor Stars and Stripes flag recognition event with fifty-thousand Boy Scouts. All this chilling activity led to pneumonia and his fatal heart attack.

As to the above mentioned Bible, Harding had rested overnight before boarding a train to San Francisco on July 27th. Worshipful Master H.L. Quigley asked the President's personal secretary, George Christian, if Bro. Harding would sign Lafayette's large Lodge Bible. Quigley offered forth the

Great Book, little suspecting the hand strokes he witnessed would be his Masonic brother's final signature.

Harding died August second while Flo, his wife, read to him. His last known request was asking a nurse for "a glass of old-fashioned blackberry juice."

Harding was traveling to Hollywood to deliver an address to Hollywood Commandery #56 of the Knights Templar and to present them with a "Traveling Banner" on behalf of his home Commandery in Marion, Ohio . Within two years of his death, six lodges had changed their names to the Warren Harding Masonic Lodge.

In addition to being Master Masons in Freemason Craft Lodges, ten presidents have sought further Masonic light.

Andrew Jackson: Accounts of the Grand Chaplain of Tennessee indicate Jackson assisted in the ceremonies of the Cumberland Chapter #1 of Royal Arch Masons.

James Knox Polk: Polk's Mark Master degree was conferred January 17, 1825, in Cumberland Chapter #1. He subsequently transferred to become a charter member of La Fayette Chapter #4 in Columbia, Tennessee, receiving his remaining degrees in April 1825, and served as Captain of the Host on September 8, 1825.

James Buchanan: Buchanan was a companion of Pennsylvania Chapter #43 of the Royal Arch in Lancaster, Pennsylvania.

Andrew Johnson: Johnson was the first President to be an active Knights Templar. Photographs exist of him in his Templar uniform. He was a member of Nashville Commandery #1 in 1859 of Nashville, Tennessee. He received his Scottish Rite Degrees in 1867, making him the first Scottish Rite President.

James Abram Garfield: Garfield received all his Capitular degrees on April 18, 1866, in Columbia Chapter #1 of the District of Columbia. He received the 14th Degree of Scottish Rite in 1872.

William McKinley, Jr.: McKinley received all his Capitular degrees on December 27-28, 1883, in Canton Chapter #84 of Ohio.

Warren Gamaliel Harding: Harding received all his Capitular degrees and Templar Orders January 11-13, 1921, in Marion Chapter #62 and Commandery #36 of Ohio. He received his Scottish Rite Degrees in 1921. Later that same year, Harding became the first President to walk the "hot sands" of the Shrine.

Franklin Delano Roosevelt: FDR became a member of the Albany Consistory of Scottish Rite of New York in 1929. He joined the Shrine in the next year.

Harry S Truman: Truman received all his Capitular degrees in Orient Chapter #102 of Kansas City, Missouri, during the four days of November 11-15, 1919. He was the 33rd President and was the first 33rd Degree Scottish Rite Mason.

Gerald Rudolph Ford: The conferral of the 33rd Degree for Bro. Ford, on September 26, 1962, took place in the Supreme Council A.A.S.R., Northern Jurisdiction at the Academy of Music in Philadelphia, Pennsylvania.

The year was 1860. The city was Buenos Aires, Argentina. The place was the altar of Union Del Plata Masonic Lodge.

Kneeling at the altar were General Justo José de Urquiza y García, Santiago Rafael Luis Manuel José María Derqui Rodríguez, Bartolomé Mitre, and Domingo Faustino Sarmiento.

Respectively, the four kneeling men represented the former third president of Argentina, the then current fourth president, the future sixth president, and the future seventh president.

General Uriquiza was originally a member of Jorge Washington Lodge #44 at Conception, Argentina, but affiliated with Union Del Plata.

While Sarmiento was Minister to the United States, he represented the Grand Lodge of Argentina and attended sessions of Grand Lodges in the States. During his political career, he was exiled from Argentina not once, but thrice. As a Mason, he was accustomed to doing things in threes.

Not all the Freemasons who have run for the presidency of the United States have been successful in their bid for the Oval Office, as evidenced by this baker's dozen:

Barry Goldwater
George McGovern
Robert Dole
Hubert H. Humphrey
Thomas E. Dewey
Alf Landon
Earl Warren
Estes Kefauver
George Wallace
John Sparkman
Wendell Wilke
Adlai Stevenson
(William Jennings Bryan beat out Adlai Stevenson for the Democratic Nomination in 1896)
William Wirt

It is well established that our first President under the US Constitution was an active Freemason. What Bro. George Washington would have found incredible is that four future

Presidents would be related to him. What would have truly astounded him is the fact that all four future relatives would also be Freemasons.

    Martin Van Buren
    Theodore Roosevelt
    William Howard Taft
    Franklin Delano Roosevelt

The most famous Volume of Sacred Law in Freemasonry is a 1767 King James Version of the Bible that belongs to St. John's Lodge #1 in New York City, New York. Founded in 1757, the Lodge was destroyed by fire in 1770. To replace the destroyed Lodge Bible, Master Jonathan Hampton presented St. John's with a heavy altar Bible printed by Mark Baskett, a London printer "By Royal Appointment to the King's Most Excellent Majesty".

The nine pound Bible contains one hundred and three steel engravings of illustrations by John Stuart, as well as, an Apocrypha, legal data, astronomical data, Biblical timeline charts, and historical maps. The deep red Moroccan leather covers are latched with a matched pair of silver clasps.

On April 30, 1789, New York Governor and Grand Master Robert R. Livingston stood in New York City Hall prepared to swear George Washington into office as President of the United States. When Livingston requested a Bible, none was to be had. Jacob Morton, the Worshipful Master of St. John's, offered to dash to the nearby Lodge and bring their Lodge Bible.

When the Bible arrived, Livingston opened it at random to Genesis 49:13, Washington placed his left palm on the right hand page, as the left page bore a set of three engravings, and Washington was sworn into office.

Four other Presidents have used this Bible for their swearing in ceremonies: Warren G. Harding, Dwight David Eisenhower, James "Jimmy" Carter, and George H.W. Bush.

George W. Bush had planned to use the Bible in 2001, but the risk of rain damage prevented its use. The Bible has been used in funeral observances for George Washington, Andrew Jackson, Zachary Taylor, and Abraham Lincoln. On July 4, 1992, the Bible was used when the USS *George Washington*, nuclear super carrier CVN-73, was commissioned.

On December 4, 1783, General George Washington gave his famous farewell address to his officers in Faunces Tavern. On September 11, 2001, the St. John's Bible was on loan in an exhibit at Faunces Tavern Museum, when terrorists attacked the World Trade Center nearby. It was two days before the Bible could be recovered under a special security escort.

New York City Hall has since been renamed Federal Hall. When not being used by St. John's for installing officers and other functions, the Bible is on display at Federal Hall. When the Bible is removed, it is always accompanied by three brothers of the St. John's Lodge, who wear white cotton gloves to handle it.

Four Presidents are known to have been sworn into office without using a Bible. Of those Presidents who used a Bible, not all of them had Bibles open to a passage of scripture. Here is a list of Presidential swearings where the use of a Bible

Harry Truman

or passage of scripture was documented.

George Washington	1789	Genesis 49:13 (randomly opened)
Martin Van Buren	1837	Proverbs 3:17

Franklin Pierce	1853	Affirmed instead of swearing No Bible used
Abraham Lincoln	1861	Randomly opened
Abraham Lincoln	1865	Matthew 7:1
Andrew Johnson	1865	Proverbs 21
Ulysses S. Grant	1873	Isaiah 11:1-3
Rutherford B. Hayes	1877	No Bible used
James A. Garfield	1881	Proverbs 21:1
Chester A. Arthur	1881	No Bible used
Grover Cleveland	1885	Psalm 112:4-10 (randomly opened)
Benjamin Harrison	1889	Psalm 121:1-6
Grover Cleveland	1893	Psalm 91:12-16
William McKinley	1897	II Chron. 1:10
William McKinley	1901	Proverbs 16
Theodore Roosevelt	1901	No Bible used
Theodore Roosevelt	1905	James 1:22-23
William Howard Taft	1909	I Kings 3:9-11
Woodrow Wilson	1913	Psalm 119
Woodrow Wilson	1917	Psalm 46
Warren G. Harding	1921	Micah 6:8 (Washington Bible)
Calvin Coolidge	1925	John 1
Herbert C. Hoover	1929	Proverbs 29:18
Franklin D. Roosevelt	1933	I Corinthians 13
Franklin D. Roosevelt	1937	I Corinthians 13
Franklin D. Roosevelt	1941	I Corinthians 13
Franklin D. Roosevelt	1945	I Corinthians 13
Harry S. Truman	1945	Closed Bible
Harry S. Truman	1949	Matthew 5:3-11
Dwight D. Eisenhower	1953	Psalm 127:1 (Washington Bible)
Dwight D. Eisenhower	1957	Psalm 33:12

John F. Kennedy	1961	Closed Bible
Lyndon B. Johnson	1963	Roman Catholic Missal Mistaken for a Bible
Lyndon B. Johnson	1965	Closed Bible
Richard M. Nixon	1969	Isaiah 2:4
Richard M. Nixon	1973	Isaiah 2:4
Gerald R. Ford	1974	Proverbs 3:5-6
James E. Carter	1977	Micah 6:8
Ronald W. Reagan	1981	II Chronicles 7:14
Ronald W. Reagan	1985	II Chronicles 7:14
George H. W. Bush	1989	Matthew 5 (Washington Bible)
William J. Clinton	1993	Galatians 6:8
William J. Clinton	1997	Isaiah 58:12
George W. Bush	2001	Closed Bible
George W. Bush	2005	randomly opened
Barack H. Obama	2009	Closed (Lincoln Bible)

Theodore Roosevelt was Governor of New York and the Vice-President-Elect when he petitioned for membership in Matinecock Lodge #806 in Glen Cove, New York. His petition was read during their November 1900 Stated Meeting. The ballot of December 12, 1900, was favorable and initiation of the candidate was calendared for January 2, 1901. Special trains of the Long Island Railroad were put into service to bring visiting Masons for the conferral that took place on the third floor of the Oyster Bay Bank building.

For the conferral of Roosevelt's Fellowcraft and Master Mason Degrees, demand was so great from visitors wishing to attend, that the Lodge issued tickets by invitation only. Even so, Roosevelt had to be raised and passed (not Masonically, but literally) hand-by-hand over the heads of the brothers in the stairway to exit the building.

Some of the men outside the Lodge were more crafty-men than fraternal Craftsmen. Among the Masons who reported having their pockets picked was the Lodge Treasurer, Captain Alfred Ludlam.

After encountering huge crowds whenever a prospective visit was announced, Roosevelt developed the habit of dropping in without providing prior notice.

Rev. Alexander G. Russell, of the Presbyterian Church at Oyster Bay, related a conversation among Masons at a White House luncheon, where Roosevelt observed, "Do you know, that the Master of my lodge is just a working man, a gardener for one of my neighbors in Oyster Bay; but when I visit Matinecock Lodge, he is my boss, and I must stand up when he orders me, and sit down when he tells me, and not speak unless he allows me."

Pulitzer Prize winning reporter Bro. John J. Leary, Jr, in his book *Talks With TR*, related a similar conversation in Indiana, "For example, when I was President, the master was Worshipful Brother Doughty (sic), gardener on the estate of one of my neighbors, and a most excellent public-spirited citizen, with whom I liked to maintain contact. Clearly I could not call upon him when I came home. It would have embarrassed him. Neither could he, without embarrassment, call on me. In the lodge it was different. He was over me, though I was President, and it was good for him and good for me to go to the Lodge, and even the folks who do not belong to or believe in the order, rather like it that I should go. They seem to feel it's part of the eternal fitness of things."

Roosevelt was referring to James Duthie, who was the head gardener for the historic Townsend Estate in Oyster Bay for many years and noted for his work with dahlias. Bro. Duthie was also the Worshipful Master of Matinecock for three of the years when Roosevelt was in office, 1902 through 1904. Among this gentlemanly Scotsman's other noteworthy accomplishments, he was: President of the Nassau County Horticultural Society, Head Usher at Christ Episcopal Church where the Roosevelts attended, and Assistant Grand Lecturer of New York.

George Washington was an irregular Mason for almost four months. Washington was born on February 22, 1732, a Julian calendar year. He was Initiated an Entered Apprentice Mason at Fredericksburg Lodge #4 of Fredericksburg, Virginia, on November 4, 1752, a Gregorian calendar year.

Accounting for the eleven days that were skipped when the United States adopted the Gregorian calendar on September 3, 1752, Washington's age at the time of his initiation was only 20 years, 8 months, and 13 days. The membership age requirement at the time was Twenty-one years of age. By the time George was Raised a Master Mason on August 4, 1753, he had reached that milestone and the irregularity of his status was cured.

When the United States ratified the Jay Treaty with England in 1796, the French considered it an unspoken declaration of America's intent to support Britain in its war with France. The ratification led to the "Quasi War" or "Franco-American War of 1798 – 1780".

On August 3, 1780, Commodore Alexander Murray, of the United States Frigate *Trumbull*, captured the armed French schooner *La Vengeance* outside the harbor of Jacquemel in the French colony of Saint-Domingue. The *La Vengeance* was taken as prize to New London, Connecticut, where her crew was imprisoned. Of the one-hundred and forty men aboard the *La Vengeance*, seventy were either naval or army officers. Seventeen of the most senior officers were held captive at Norwich, Connecticut, eighty-four prisoners were taken to Hartford under militia guard, and the remaining prisoners were detained in the New London jail.

A most unusual Army Lieutenant by the name of Jean Pierre Boyer was among the prisoners held at Norwich. Boyer was the twenty-four year old *"gens de couleur"* or black-mulatto son of a French father and an African slave mother. When captured, he had in his possession a collection of Masonic catechisms for all Degrees from Entered Apprentice through Perfect Master, a Charter from the Grand Orient in Paris, numerous other Masonic documents and records, and a complete set of officers' jewels, aprons, collars, and cuffs.

Somerset Lodge #34 of Norwich was Chartered in 1794. When the brothers of Somerset determined that the young Lieutenant Boyer was in fact a Freemason, they secured his transfer from the jail to the home of Brother Diah Manning. Somerset Lodge authorized an allowance for Boyer's room, board, and necessities during his confinement. They welcomed him into their Lodge and coached him in mastering his English. When America's undeclared war with France ended, the brothers of Somerset made sure Boyer did not return to St. Domingue empty handed.

Between 1818 and 1843, Bro. Jean Pierre Boyer was better known to his brothers at Somerset by a new title, the President of Haiti.

Alexander Kaufman Coney was born on April Fool's Day 1848, in Athens. Not the one in Greece, but the Athens near Shreveport, Louisiana. His father was a German immigrant and his mother was Louisa Lee of "The Virginia Lees". As a young man, he was a pharmacist in New York City and was Raised in Silentia Lodge #198 of that city on February 24, 1875.

City life was not to his liking, and the next year he was the purser aboard the SS *City of Havana*. Meanwhile, General Porfirio Díaz was overthrown at the disastrous Battle of Icamole. He attempted to re-enter Mexico by sailing from New Orleans aboard the *City of Havana*. During the voyage, he claimed to be a Cuban physician by the name of Dr. De La Boza. When the ship stopped in Tampico to take aboard a battalion of government troops, Díaz believed he had been discovered and attempted to swim to shore. A long boat was launched, and he was rescued from certain death. But his identity became known to the soldiers. Back aboard the ship, he claimed protection under the ship's American flag. This was granted, but only until the ship reached Vera Cruz, where Díaz would be turned over to the local military and shot.

Díaz requested assistance from Bro. Coney in helping him swim to shore, but was convinced that this was foolhardy. Instead, the purser tossed a ship's life-saving buoy overboard with some of the General's clothes. The splash resulted in another long boat being launched, but the General's body could not be found. A diligent search was made of the ship, but no account of the General could be discovered.

Little did the commander of the troops realize that when he played cards at night in the purser's cabin during the remainder of the voyage, that he was sitting on a sofa with the General hidden inside a concealed cavity.

With Coney's help, Díaz rejoined the rebels. He regained victory and became President of Mexico for twenty-seven years. As President, he appointed Coney as Mexico's Consul General to St. Nazaire, France, and later as Consul General to the Republic of the United States in San Francisco.

While in San Francisco, Bro. Coney joined Royal Arch and Scottish Rite Masonry. He was the Grand Representative of the Gran Dieta Simbolica of the Republic of Mexico to the Grand Lodge of California, and Chairman of the Masonic Relief Board.

Coney joined San Francisco's French language La Loge La Parfaite Union Lodge #17 and was its Master for two years. La Parfaite Union holds the distinction of being the first foreign language Lodge to be formed in California.

After leaving the service of Mexico, Coney applied for restoration of his American citizenship, which was granted. He was buried by his San Francisco Masonic brothers in 1930 with the title, "The Mason who saved the Republic of Mexico".

Both Masonic and anti-Masonic conspiracy theorists oftentimes cite that President Ronald Wilson Reagan was a Freemason. He wasn't. The confusion arises from a ceremony that took place in the Oval Office on February 11, 1988.

Grand Master Raymond F. McMullen of the District of Columbia presented the President with a "Certificate of Honor". According to the certificate, Reagan's life was a testament to the Masonic principles of Brotherly Love, Relief, and Truth. This certificate should not to be confused with a Grand Master making a man a Mason-at-Sight.

Also present at the ceremony were Sovereign Grand Commander Francis S. Paul of the Northern Masonic Jurisdiction of Scottish Rite and Sovereign Grand Commander C. Fred Kleinknecht of the Southern Jurisdiction of Scottish Rite, who jointly presented Reagan with a diploma that "Conferred the title of Honorary Scottish Rite Mason" on the President.

Imperial Potentate Voris King of the Ancient Arabic Order of the Nobles of the Mystic Shrine presented a framed certificate to the President that made him an "Honorary Member of the Imperial Council" of the A.A.O.N.M.S..

Both Scottish Rite and the Shrine are concordant bodies to Freemason Craft Lodges and have neither authority nor jurisdiction to confer the title or position of Freemason on any man. Apparently, this was not explained to the President, for on February 22, 1988, he wrote the following, thanking Grand Commander Kleinknecht, "... for the framed certificate of membership, ... (I am) honored to join the ranks of sixteen former Presidents in their association with Freemasonry." Reagan attended and participated in both Scottish Rite and Shrine events as President, but was never admitted into a Blue Lodge of Freemasons.

As a Masonic footnote, for a brief period later in the year, Grand Master McMullen suspended Grand Commander Keinknecht of all the rights and benefits of a Freemason. It took mediation by the Grand Master of Maryland before Keinknecht acknowledged the primacy of the Grand Lodge of the District of Columbia within its jurisdiction, and the Grand Commander's rights and benefits in Freemasonry were restored.

Between 1774 and the adoption of the Constitution, the United States was governed by the Continental Congress. The Articles of Confederation were adopted in 1781, and John Hanson was elected "President of the United States under Congress Assembled". There are many who believe Hanson deserves recognition as the first President of the United States and George Washington as the first President under the Constitution.

There were fourteen men who served as President prior to Washington. They are sometimes referred to as America's Secret Presidents or Unknown Presidents, because so few Americans know anything about them. Four of these fourteen were Freemasons. Here is their Masonic history.

Peyton Randolph took office on September 5, 1774, as the first president of the Congress, but his term lasted less than two months due to poor health. Henry Middleton took the office until Randolph returned in May of 1775. But ailing health again forced him out of office after two weeks. He died later in the year, never seeing the creation of the Declaration of Independence. Randolph was the last Provisional Grand Master of Virginia.

John Hancock assumed the role of fourth President when Randolph left office for the second time. He served until the end of October 1777 and again in November 1785 through June 1786. The well liked merchant is best remembered for his prominent signature on the Declaration of Independence. He was Initiated and Raised a Mason in Marchant Lodge #277 of Quebec, Canada, in 1762. In Boston, he became a member of St. Andrew's Lodge.

Henry Laurens was the fifth President from November 1777 until December 1778. The South Carolinian had amassed his wealth as the proprietor of the largest slave trading operation in North America. In 1779, Congress appointed him Minister to the Netherlands. He negotiated an agreement with the Dutch guaranteeing their support for the colonies against Britain. During his return voyage, he was captured and returned to London. He was the only American ever imprisoned in the Tower of London. Which is ironic in light of his occupation as an importer of captive slaves. Richard Oswald, a former business partner, negotiated Laurens release in exchange for General Lord Cornwallis. In 1783, Congress appointed Laurens to the commission negotiating the Treaty of Paris. One of the men on the British side of the table was Richard Oswald. Laurens's son had advocated the release of slaves, but had been killed during the war before they were freed. After the war, Laurens freed his son's slaves. Laurens was a member of Solomon Lodge # 1 in South Carolina and had been its Grand Steward in 1754. Upon his death, he became the first man to be cremated for burial in America.

Brigadier General Arthur St. Clair was the thirteenth pre-Washington President. He served from February 1787 through November of that year. He resigned to assume a post as Governor of the Northwest Territory. While living in the Ohio Territory, he signed the petition to Charter the Lodge Nova Caesarea Harmony #2 in Cincinnati, and the Tyler's book records his attendance in the Lodge. Military Lodge records were frequently lost or destroyed during wartime. The Lodge where Bro. St.Clair was Raised is unknown.

CHAPTER 21

THE HIGH AND THE LOW

The early meetings of ancient Operative Masons took place in temples not made with hands, secluded locations such as quarries, mountain tops, and forests. Later, these working men met in guild buildings, pubs, taverns, and homes. In modern times, many Speculative Freemasons have rediscovered the spirituality and joy of outdoor Degrees and novel locations. Some of these meetings, convocations, and ritual work are described in the following pages.

There is an ancient truism that the three cardinal rules of real estate are: location, location, and location. Many Lodges have made due with locations that were thrust upon them by circumstances of history and geography. Other Lodges, like Lodge #239 of Paris, France, have embraced the novelty of remote locations.

The date was August 23, 1879. The purpose of the Lodge meeting was the initiation of a new brother. The place was Paris, France. The Degree was not exactly conferred "in" the city as one might expect, but five hundred feet above Paris in a hot air balloon, by three officers and the candidate. Remaining Lodge brethren stood on the level ground below.

Conspiracy theorists will go crazy over this fact. On March 9, 1822, a Masonic conference was held in Washington, D.C., in the chambers of The United States Senate.

The meeting was called by none other than Henry Clay. The Henry Clay who was Secretary of State under John Quincy Adams, a US Senator, a US Congressman, Speaker of the House, Republican Presidential Candidate, and a duelist, as well as an active Freemason. W. Bro. Clay was Master of Lexington Lodge #1, Grand Orator of the Grand Lodge of Kentucky, and in 1820 was Grand Master of Kentucky.

At issue in the 1822 meeting was the formation of a National Masonic Grand Lodge. The invitees were "Those members of Congress who belong to the Masonic Fraternity, and those visitors to the city who are or have been members of any State Grand Lodge are respectfully invited to attend a meeting, to be held in the Senate Chamber."

W. Bro. Thomas R. Ross of Ohio was elected Chairman of the meeting. A Member of Congress from Pennsylvania, Bro. William Darlington, was appointed Secretary. The meeting was called to order promptly at seven. This was the only fraternal meeting ever held in either chamber of Congress.

On June 3, 1938, brothers of the Irish Military Lodge of the Worcestershire Regiment were on duty as guards at a British landmark. Their Lodge, Glittering Star Lodge #322 Initiated a candidate within the Tower of London.

The Masonic Lodge in Bishop, California, was granted its dispensation on June 20, 1887. Three proposed names had been advanced for Lodge #287, New Hope Lodge, Valley Lodge, and Winnedumah Lodge. Because of Bishop's proximity to Death Valley, Valley Lodge was the presumed favorite. There was an obvious new hope for the future with those brothers who had settled in Bishop. But, California Grand Secretary Abell selected Winnedumah because of a local Indian legend. What was the influential legend?

Many moons had passed as grandfathers passed the story of two brothers down to their grandsons, generation after generation. The great Warrior-Chief Tinnemaha and the tribe's Medicine Man Winnedumah found their tribe in a pickle of a battle with an enemy tribe. Tinnemaha sent his brother to ascend the Inyo Ridge and invoke the blessing of The Great Spirit in the forthcoming fight.

Alas, Tinnemaha was slain. Faithful to his cause, Winnedumah stayed his post, waiting in vain for his brother and word of victory. His was a tenacious and steadfast spirit of great proportion. So great and steadfast was Winnedumah, that he turned into the stone known as the Winnedumah Paiute Monument. It is an eight foot monolith that stands mid-way between Waucoba Mountain and Mount Inyo at an elevation of 8,369 feet.

But, our story deals with an event that was much lower than the monument. On April 10, 1936, Winnedumah Lodge #287 held a ritual on the floor of Death Valley. At 270 feet below sea level, Death Valley is the lowest surface spot in North America. Masons were present from more than fifty Lodges and eleven states were represented. The standing joke at the "Furnace Creek" site was that all the visiting brothers were "warmly greeted".

Captain M. LeTellier of the whaling ship *Ajax* held a commission from the Supreme Council Thirty-third Degree of France "... to set up Lodges in the Pacific Ocean and elsewhere in his voyages to issue warrants, to call upon the Supreme Council for charters, and to make Masons at sight ...". On April 8, 1842, he formed the first lodge of the Missouri River. The ritual was in French, the degrees were the first three degrees of

Scottish Rite Masonry, the location was Honolulu, and the Lodge was aboard the deck of his whaling ship. The Lodge was later named *Le Progres de L'Oceanie #124* under the jurisdiction of The Grand Lodge of Hawaii.

We have now read of a Lodge at sea level and one below sea level. Both of these were on the surface of land, now comes some that were below the surface. Not all locations have been safe. The Grand Lodge of Arizona met in the depths of Copper Queen Cave of Bisbee, Arizona, November 9-13, 1897. A few months later, the mammoth chamber collapsed.

Volcano Lodge #56 in Amador County, California, was organized in 1853. Its first five meetings were held in a cave that is called Volcano Masonic Cave.

The original two story Lodge building was constructed of quarried limestone blocks. The first story was built to allow horses to be stabled on the ground floor. This was but one of the safety measures. Another was that there was no outside fire escape. To keep out eavesdroppers and attackers, each floor had a heavy door made of iron that was barred from within. Wood joists were sheathed in copper, and the roof was covered with a layer of coarse sand to reduce the risk of fire from flaming arrows and hurled torches. The reason for the fortress-like construction was to make it a stronghold against commonplace raiders such as Joaquin Carrillo Murrieta.

In 1972, the Master of Union Lodge #38 of Kingston, Tennessee, wanted to hold an outdoor degree. Eblen's Cave, eight miles from Kingston on the farm of Clayton Brashears, seemed a perfect location, and Mr. Brashears was approached. Not only did he agree that they could use the cave in 1972, but it became an annual affair drawing masons from around the country and from foreign soil.

Each year, a degree and ritual team was selected from a different Lodge or jurisdiction. As an example, the August 21, 1993, team from Mission Bay Lodge #771 of San Diego, California, conferred a Master Mason Degree on Richard Knight. Mission Bay's Lodge Secretary was seated in the East as the obligating Master because he was the candidate's father. Present were 327 Master Masons from 112 Lodges, representing twenty states and Germany.

Neither Farmer Clayton Brashears nor any member of his family was a mason until 2009, when a grandson became a member of Vonore Lodge #658 in Vonore, Tennessee.

Robert Burns Masonic Lodge #97 of Burns, Oregon, owns the lava tube Malheur Cave. In 1938, Ulysses S. Hackney and Charles Logan presented the idea of conferring a degree inside the cave.

On October 1, 1938, following a "Buckaroo" dinner, a Master Mason degree was conferred on William Merle Bennett and witnessed by brothers from twenty-one Lodges representing seven states.

The cave is shallow in height, varying between seven and twenty feet, and approximately thirty football fields deep in length.

The event was such a success, that it has been maintained as an annual August tradition.

Me'arat Tzedkiyahu or Zekekiah's Cave was discovered in Palestine in 1854. The cave has been used for Masonic work as far back as May 13, 1868, when Robert Morris, Past Grand Master of the Grand Lodge of Kentucky, conducted the first ritual work in Palestine. In attendance were: the British Captain and officers from H.M.S. *Lord Clyde* that was berthed in Jaffa; the Governor of Jaffa, Noureddin Effendi, who was a member of Lodge Amitie Clemente of Paris; American Vice-Consul, R. Beardsley; and Henry Petermann, the Consul of Prussia to Jerusalem.

Meetings were suspended in 1948, when the Old City of Jerusalem was captured by Jordan's Arab Legion, and the tunnels to the cavern were sealed. Degree work resumed in 1969, when the Supreme Grand Royal Arch Masons of the State of Israel held a Mark Master degree. The cave is believed to be part of the original King Solomon's quarries.

It should be noted for both Biblical and Masonic reference that the quarrying of stone is far enough underground that the sounds of metal tools cannot be heard at the site of King Solomon's Temple (I Kings 6:7).

There have been Mark Master Degrees through Royal Arch Degrees conferred in Zekehiah's Cave every year since 1969.

Martin's Station Lodge #188 of Virginia conferred a Master Mason degree in 1954 in Cudjo's Cave. The ritual was held 952 feet below the surface of a Cumberland Mountain between the cities of Cumberland Gap, Tennessee and Middleburo, Kentucky. There were 345 Masons present representing over a dozen Virginian Lodges.

Numerous "Cave Meetings" have been held by Lodges in Kentucky's Mammoth Cave at 135 feet underground. The same is true for New Mexico's Carlsbad Caverns at 750 feet underground.

Circumstances beyond the Master's control may necessitate the moving of a meeting or degree, thus it was in 1928 at Culver City-Foshay Masonic Lodge #467, a stone's throw to the south of Beverly Hills, California.

The original Foshay Lodge was built in 1917, on Cardiff Avenue. By 1928, the brethren needed more space and had constructed a two-story Lodge on Venice Boulevard.

A special communication was held by the Grand Lodge of California to lay the ceremonial cornerstone on November 10, 1928. The Lodge Room and stairwell was filled beyond standing-room only capacity. In attendance with the Grand Lodge officers and Foshay brethren, there was a multitude of visitors from throughout Southern California.

After a street procession to the Lodge, a sizeable crowd had assembled. Lodge Tiler Herbert P. Nathan found it necessary to have "deputized Assistant Tylers" to "keep the visiting ladies away from the proceedings".

Masonic wives and widows, as well as, ladies of the community are invited to attend cornerstone ceremonies, so why were they a problem on November tenth? The Grand Master deemed the Lodge Room "too small" to accommodate the ceremony. Taking his officers with him, they had "retired to the Ladies' powder room to open Grand Lodge".

Between 1862 and 1865, Lodges in Nevada met under Charters from the Grand Lodge of California. The Grand Lodge of Nevada was formed in 1865 in Carson City.

All was well until a fire in 1875 gutted the building of records and library.

During the rebuilding process, Grand Lodge held a meeting with 378 in attendance at 7,827 above sea level atop Mount Davidson.

According to the Grand Lodge of the State of Israel, "The first Masonic Lodge in the Holy Land was the Royal Solomon Mother Lodge No. 293, under the Grand Lodge of Canada in Ontario, whose first meeting was held in the King Solomon's Quarries of Jerusalem on May 7, 1873." Before that, an "occasional assembly" of Masons performed a Secret Monitor ceremony in the same location on May 13, 1868.

St. Patrick's Day in Boston is always a day of special events. March 17, 1926, was no exception. On that St. Paddy's Day, the Major General Henry Knox Masonic Lodge was constituted in the Charleston Navy Yard of Boston aboard "Old Ironsides", the American frigate USS *Constitution*.

Lodge Jamrud #4372 held a meeting in a "Mohammedan village near the Khyber Pass". A British Major, who attended the 1935 ritual, told of earthen heaps serving as pedestals, altar, benches, and officers' chairs. Tent mallets and pick handles served as gavels and rods. No degrees were conferred, and the Lodge "was closed before dusk".

In Oregon, an outdoor meeting had to be tiled by a Sheriff's posse composed of Masons on horseback. Likewise in Marietta, Ohio, there were mounted Tilers stationed around the rim of a deep quarry, who would call out their reports that the Lodge was securely Tiled (guarded).

Nation Lodge #566 in Spencerville, Ottawa, Canada, has conducted degree work in the nearby quarry on John Hunter's farm west of Highway 416. W. Bro. Hunter is a Past District Deputy Grand Master for the St. Lawrence District. He is the sixth generation to own the land. Besides the quarry, there are 1,200 maple trees from which the Hunters produce syrup.

An eight-hundred pound slab of rough limestone resting atop large logs serves as an altar. Squared blocks of limestone serve as Officers' chairs and cut timber acts as pedestals and pillars. A small travel trailer acts as the Preparation Room for candidates.

The Tiler is aided in his duties by the remoteness of the site and by a cadre of men acting as sentinels on the lone road into the quarry site, as well as, men posted about the rim of the twenty acre quarry.

Lodge fires were common in the 1800s. As a result of one such fire in 1803, a most unusual Lodge was created.

The Masons of Derby, Vermont, built Lively Stone Lodge #22 in 1803. The Lodge was near the Canadian border, and Masons from nearby Stanstead would frequent the meetings in Derby. When Lively Stone burned that year, both sets of Masons found themselves without a home Lodge. Their solution was to build a Lodge that was transected by the border between the United States and Canada.

The new Golden Lodge #5 had two entry doors into the assembly area, one door opened into Canada and one door opened into the United States.

All went well until 1812, when the two countries found themselves at war. The men of Stanstead completed construction of Golden Rule Lodge #19 in 1813. This didn't prevent communication between the two groups, as Lodge records indicate there were still "fraternal" meetings thanks to tavern keeper Bro. Adam Noyes and the convenience of his establishment.

In terms of unusual locations, Golden Rule had more to offer than a transected building. Beginning in 1857, the renumbered Golden Rule Lodge #5 held annual mountaintop services on Owl's Head Mountain. The early attendees didn't have the current advantage of a ski lift for part of their 2,580 foot ascension to the Owl's Head summit.

Atop Owl's Head in Quebec, visitors from throughout Canada, America, New Zealand, Australia, Europe, and Asia have beheld the breathtaking view of mountains in New

Hampshire and Vermont, as well as, the beautiful glacially formed Lake Memphremagog, as it's called on the Vermont shore or Lac Memphrémagog, as it's called on the Quebec shore.

In 1782, Capt. George Smith was the cause of much debate and the changing of the Constitution of the Grand Lodge of England. It seems that Bro. Smith was visiting prisons and "Initiating" the prisoners as Entered Apprentice Masons.

Grand Lodge took a dim view of this clandestine behavior and changed the Constitution in 1784 to read, "It is inconsistent with the principles of Freemasonry for any Freemason Lodge to be held for the purpose of making, passing, or raising any Masons in any prison or place of confinement." The Grand Master emphasized that only a "Free man" could enter Freemasonry.

It took a short boat trip, but on July 8, 2006, the brethren of Corner Stone Lodge of Duxbury, Massachusetts and Plymouth Lodge of Plymouth, Massachusetts held a shared conferral of three Fellowcraft Degrees on Clark's Island.

Clark's Island is historically significant because the Pilgrims landed there before proceeding on to Plymouth. Some people claim that the prominent Bishop's Rock on the island is the true Plymouth Rock. Henry David Thoreau wrote of the island in his 1851 journal, "This island contains about 86 acres and was once covered with red cedars which were sold at Boston for gate posts-I saw a few left-one 2 foot in diameter at the ground-which was probably standing when the pilgrims came."

Clark's Island has been owned by Bro. Skip Watson Taylor's family since the 1600s.

At the 2006 gathering, Corner Stone's ritual team conferred degrees on three candidates (Two from Corner Stone and one from Plymouth), and two fifty-year pins were presented.

Kerosene lanterns sitting atop empty whiskey barrels acted as the three lesser lights. The altar was made of wood from the *Mayflower II*.

While the Master was in top hat and tails, others were barefoot and wore shorts. The timing of the ceremonies was critical in order to avoid their departing at low tide.

Palmer Lodge #372 of Fort Erie was chartered in 1879. The Canadian fort by the same name was established in 1766.

The original fort was protected by a moat, a drawbridge, and a four-inch thick solid "hard oak" door.

Beginning in 2001, Palmer Lodge has obtained permission from the Niagara Parks Commission to confer degrees within the Fort's grounds. The rituals are attended by brethren wearing 1812 period uniforms and current Canadian Forces servicemen in modern uniforms. In 1812, the Americans were invaders; today, they are invitees.

During the Civil War, the Union Army had ninety-four military Lodges; the Confederacy had ninety-two.

During World War One, there were ten American military Lodges in the European Theater of Operations (ETO) and three military Lodges stateside.

During World War Two, the United States Army had none, but the Irish had five.

Charleston Masonic Lodge #35 of Charleston, Illinois, was a "Moon Lodge". It held its stated meetings not on a monthly basis, but on the "Tuesday next after the full moon".

Until October 1845, this Coles County Lodge was named "The Morning Star Lodge". Their Ohio Charter changed the name of the Lodge because there was a Morning Star Lodge #30 already existing in Canton, Ohio.

Charleston's Morning Star Lodge held their regular Moon Lodge communications in "thick and dense hazel thickets south of Charleston proper". After receiving their Charter, they began meetings in a small log cabin, not as much for formality, as it was for weather. The rawness of winter's cold was biting in the hazel thicket.

The highest elevation Lodge is Roof of the World Lodge #1094 in Cerro de Pasco, Peru, at 14,208 feet. It was Chartered in 1912 by the Grand Lodge of Scotland. The Lodge is on the side of Mount Meiggs. The brethren have held meetings and Degree conferrals atop the Mount at an altitude of 17,575 feet.

When formed by engineers and executives from mining consortiums, the brothers could only travel the rough and rugged road to the Lodge by foot or on the backs of llamas.

Craft Lodges are not the only Masons to hold rituals under a canopy of stars.

In Washington, Centralia Chapter #44 and Sunset Chapter #23 have held Royal Arch Mason pageants in the Tenino sandstone quarry. Two of the pageants that received statewide attention were August 5, 1950, and August 4, 1951.

The class of new companions in 1950 was comprised of over one hundred men, and the class of 1951 of over sixty men. The officers presenting the degrees wore white overalls and used natural materials for the altar and chairs deep within the massive walls of the quarry. At times, the annual event has drawn over five hundred Royal Arch companions from Chapters in Washington and Oregon.

Blocks from Tenino were used to construct the original State Capitol in Olympia.

A commemorative slab from Tenino is found at the 310 foot level of the Washington Monument.

While on the topic of the Washington Monument, the limestone commemorative slab found at the 110 foot level on the ninth landing came from a quarry just south of Utica, New York. The famous carvers of stone monuments, Owens & Newland, prepared the plaque that bears a "Square and Compass with G" in the lower left quarter.

The same quarry was the site of conferrals by Oneida Chapter #57 on May 16, 1953. The event was noteworthy in that it received a full-page of coverage in the Utica newspaper.

Riverside Chapter #67 of California was established in 1886, but didn't venture out-of-doors until 1932. In that year, they started an annual pageant atop the 1,329 foot Mount Rubidoux.

The groups were modest until after the World War Two, when the class of new companions jumped to sixty on April 2, 1947. What was more remarkable was that the sideliners represented Royal Arch Masons from fourteen states.

Mount Rubidoux is noted in Southern California for its Easter Sunrise Services that began when Teddy Roosevelt was President and the annual Fourth of July fireworks display.

What do casinos and Masonry have in common? The answer is the Colorado River Fall Festival. Each October, York Rite Masons from across the nation and beyond our borders come for the annual pageant that includes all the Degrees and Orders of the Chapter, the Council, and the Commandery.

The popular festival started in 1991 in Arizona. In 1993, it moved to Harrah's Casino in Nevada. In 1998, it moved to its current location, Riverside Hotel and Casino in Laughlin, Nevada. While the Companions and Sir Knights confer Degrees on the candidates in the Starview Room overlooking the Colorado River, their ladies are a floor below at the slot machines and gaming tables. Each year there are candidates from Arizona, California, Nevada, New Mexico, and Utah. There have been candidates from other states and countries such as Ecuador, Paraguay, and the Netherlands.

The Royal Arch Chapter of Weeping Water, Nebraska, conferred degrees on 81 new companions in 1953. The location was in a local quarry. Five hundred and twenty-one companions representing twenty-three different Chapters witnessed the event. But Nebraska was outdone by Kansas, as the next article relates.

Do you know the secret Masonic password "Kanorado" and its significance to a joke between two Lodge brothers?

There was a Masonic gathering for the week of August 6 through 13, A. Dep. 2899 (That's 1899 for most of us). The gathering required two railways to add special trains and sleepers from Chicago and the Eastern seaboard. There were so many Masons on the trains that men were specially assigned to direct seating and berth assignments.

The Masons were coming from Kansas, Massachusetts, South Carolina, Tennessee, Wyoming, Nebraska, Missouri,

Maryland, Ohio, New York, Minnesota, Rhode Island, Virginia, Louisiana, and Colorado. Those from Colorado had the shortest distance to travel as their destination was near the base of Pike's Peak.

The event started as a joke in Kansas and finished as an awesome week in Colorado. Ellsworth Council #9 of Cryptic Masons in Ellsworth, Kansas, had to cancel the winter conferral on their local candidates because a blizzard was underway, and the mountains of snow were impossible to traverse. A companion jokingly commented that it would be easier to haul everyone to Colorado in the summer than to traverse the deep snow banks blocking the Lodge. Word got out about the seed of truth in the joke. Serious interest took root, and enthusiasm for the idea began to grow.

The August 10, 1899, conferral of Royal Master, Select Master, and Super Excellent Master Degrees atop the 14,127 foot summit of Pike's Peak had a class of 206 candidates and hundreds of companions from fifteen states.

On the eleventh, a ceremony was conducted placing a bronze historical marker on the Peak to commemorate the event. It is an inscribed triangle having sides measuring two-feet each. The week was capped off with a banquet of turtle soup and clams.

As to the password, so many men needed to be examined to make sure they were current members of councils, a committee of "two-councils" or fifty-four companions was formed under a "Conductor of the Council". As each companion qualified, he was presented with a specially minted badge suspended by a pin and ribbon to commemorate the event, a registration number, and the password "KANORADO", representing KAN for Kansas and ORADO for Colorado.

The Lodge of Regeneration was established as the Grand Lodge of Portugal aboard the HMS *Phoenix* while it was in Lisbon in 1797. Government efforts to suppress Freemasonry included imprisonment and exile. In 1810, thirty of the major leaders in Portuguese Freemasonry were sentenced to exile in the Azores. Despite the government's effort, Masonry continued to grow. In 1812, there were more than a dozen Lodges just in Lisbon.

We finish this chapter with a visit to the most remote location related to Freemasonry. The date of the singular event was July 20, 1969.

Command Module Pilot Michael Collins orbited in *Columbia*, while Neil Armstrong and Bro. Edwin Eugene "Buzz" Aldrin landed the *Eagle* in the Sea of Tranquility (*Mare Tranquilitatis)* on the lunar surface.

Aldrin was a member of Clear Lake Lodge #1417 of Seabrook, Texas. When he stepped onto the non-terrestrial dust, Bro. Aldrin carried a Special Deputation of the Grand Lodge of Texas issued by Grand Master J. Guy Smith. The Special Deputation granted Aldrin the authority to claim "Masonic Territorial Jurisdiction" for "The Most Worshipful Grand Lodge of Texas, Ancient Free and Accepted Masons, on The Moon".

In commemoration of Bro. Aldrin's unique Masonic event, Texas chartered Tranquility Lodge #2000, "for the purpose of promoting, encouraging, conducting and fostering the principles of Freemasonry, and to assist in promoting the health, welfare, education and patriotism of children worldwide."

Tranquility holds an Annual Meeting in Waco each July with quarterly meetings held in diverse Lodges throughout Texas, until such time as a meeting can be held on the lunar surface.

CHAPTER 22

RENAISSANCE MASON

"Freemasonry has tenets peculiar to itself. They serve as testimonials of character and qualifications, which are only conferred after due course of instruction and examination. These are of no small value; they speak a universal language, and act as a passport to the attentions and support of the initiated in all parts of the world. They cannot be lost as long as memory retains its power.

Let the possessor of them be expatriated, shipwrecked or imprisoned, let him be stripped of everything he has got in the world, still those credentials remain, and are available for use as circumstances require.

The good effects they have produced are established by the most incontestable facts of history. They have stayed the uplifted hand of the destroyer; they have softened the asperities of the tyrant; they have mitigated the horrors of captivity; they have subdued the rancor of malevolence; and broken down the barriers of political animosity and sectarian alienation. On the field of battle, in the solitudes of the uncultivated forest, or in the busy haunts of the crowded city, they have made men of the most hostile feelings, the most distant regions, and diversified conditions, rush to the aid of each other, and feel a special joy and satisfaction that they have been able to afford relief to a Brother Mason." Benjamin Franklin, Philadelphia

These words by Brother Benjamin Franklin help us understand why men join the fraternity of Freemasonry.

Within these pages we have shared the stories of interesting Masons; the highs and lows of extraordinary men who did ordinary things, and ordinary men who did extraordinary things. We finish the book with a tribute to one Mason, an extraordinary man who did extraordinary things.

Henry "Hank" M. Wheeler was only two when his father, a stock drover, moved his family westward to the frontier town of Northfield in the Minnesota Territory. The year was 1856. As a youngster, Henry's mastery of hunting skills helped to feed the family. While in Northfield, his mother, Huldah, bore a daughter and another son. In due time, his father purchased a drug store in the growing town, a move which gave the scholarly boy access to books and information about medicine.

After Henry graduated from the fledgling Carleton College, he applied to and was accepted at the prestigious University of Michigan Medical School. The young man was on the path to becoming a simple country doctor, but the "Northfield Gunfight" of September 7, 1876, altered his travel plans.

On that fateful day, Henry was helping at this father's store. He was on the front landing, when he observed the "Jesse James and Cole Younger Gang" ride into town to rob the First National Bank. It was the vacationing Henry who raised the hue and cry by shouting, "Grab your guns, they're robbing the Bank!"

Henry's warning prompted the outlaw Clell Miller to hastily take a wild shot at the young man. If Miller had taken time to aim, the twists in this story would have been quite different.

Henry ducked into the two-story Dampier Hotel next to his father's store and ran to a second floor window. On his way forth, he grabbed a worn Sharps cavalry carbine and its meager stock of three rounds of ammunition from behind the hotel counter.

With their ill-planned robbery having gone awry and two unarmed townsfolk dead, the twarted gang tried to make their empty-handed escape. But, the dauntless medical student had other ideas. Henry's first shot hit Jim Younger in the shoulder, turning him around in the saddle as he rode pass.

Clell Miller was prepared to shoot Elias Stacy in the back, when Henry's second shot knocked Miller out of his saddle. It wasn't the fall that killed the outlaw, it the artery Henry's shot had severed.

With only one round remaining, Henry took his time before firing. The twenty-two year old spotted a six-shooter protruding from behind a staircase across the street. The gun was aimed at the local hardware dealer, Anselm Manning. Relying on his hunting skills and knowledge of anatomy, Henry lifted the tired carbine to his shoulder and shattered Bob Younger's right elbow with his sole remaining bullet, saving Anselm's life.

As they say in movie westerns, "When the dust settled" two of the desperados lay dead on the dirt. Being a practical young man, Henry asked the Sheriff to send the cadavers to the medical college. The old Sheriff is reported to have replied, *"Hank, it would be against the law for me to turn the bodies over to you, but I'll tell you what, I'll see that the outlaws are buried plenty shallow."*

Two fellow medical students were sharing their vacations with Wheeler, Edward "Eddie" Dampier (whose father owned the hotel from whence Henry fired) and Clarence Edward Persons. Three days after the shootout, the three young men delivered two bodies to a farmer outside of town. Needing time to obtain the proper chemicals for shipping, the bodies were stored in a tin-lined pickling trough used for salting pork. A week later, two odiferous barrels arrived at the college. Accounts differ as to whether the barrels bore painted labels reading, "FRESH PAINT" or "PICKLES".

Henry married his high school sweetheart. He did advanced studies at the College of Physicians and Surgeons in New York City before setting up a practice in Northfield. The next year, his wife died in childbirth, and their sickly newborn died shortly thereafter. Heartbroken, Henry left Northfield for Grand Forks, North Dakota.

Dr. Wheeler was the official Railway Surgeon for both the Great Northern Railway and the Northern Pacific Railway. He was President of the North Forks Gun Club, the North Dakota State Medical Board, the Pioneer Club, and the Whist Club. He was an officer in the Elks, the Knights of Pythias, the Odd Fellows, the Commercial Club (a precursor to the Chamber of Commerce), and the United States Pension Board.

He was active in national and local politics. He was the State campaign manager for fellow Mason, President William McKinley. He was the three time Mayor of Grand Forks.

With all this community involvement, he still found time to be Master of Acacia Lodge #15 (three times), Grand Junior Warden, Grand Deputy Master (twice), and Grand Master, as well as, fulfilling duties in the Shrine and all Orders of York Rite Masonry.

After his second wife died in 1914, the whole community grieved with their friend. For many years, Henry was the sole occupant of the beautiful home that is now on the National Registry of Historical Buildings.

Stories abound of Wheeler making house calls to families in need. If the family had no money to pay his bill, it was common to discover that "Doctor Hank" had left money behind for food and medicine.

Years passed for the twice widowed and childless gentleman. In 1925, he married a Miss Mae McCullock. A year later, Henry Jr. was born. In celebration of the birth, the seventy-one year old father raised a flag over City Hall. In his excitement, Wheeler failed to realize that he had raised the flag in the inverted position, the universal naval signal of a ship in distress. This gave his friends a chuckle.

Henry's time with his son was less than either would have liked. Four years later, the Knights Templar served as Honor Guards when the Doc's memorial was performed by Acacia Lodge. But, this was not to be his only Masonic service.

It was necessary for the railroad to attach additional passenger cars when the train brought Henry's body back to Northfield. With a multitude of his friends in attendance, the last among the participants in the 1876 shootout, received Masonic internment next to his childhood sweetheart and parents.

Throughout Henry's life, he lived up to both the ideals of his beloved fraternity, as well as, his middle name.

Dr. Henry Mason Wheeler

We end with the story of a "lifelong" Mason, or the closest thing thereto? Samuel E. Adams from Vermont rented the top floor of his Monticello, Minnesota, general store to Monticello Lodge #16. When Mrs. Adams went into labor on September 15, 1861, Doctor James W. Mulvaney moved her from her small living quarters into the upstairs Lodge Room. Henry Rice Adams was born later that night. It was in this same Lodge Room of his birth that Henry took his first steps as a Freemason in February 1864.

Henry, an agent with MC Wilcox Insurance, moved in 1885 and affiliated with Minneapolis Lodge #19. He married Cora Belle Kreis in July 1886. In 1898, he was the charter Master of Minnesota Lodge #224 in Bloomington and was Grand Master of the Minnesota Grand Lodge for 1903 - 1904. On March 30, 1928, while attending his Lodge, he suffered a fatal heart attack. Henry Rice Adams is the only man known to have been born, Raised, and died in a Masonic Lodge Room.

GLOSSARY

LODGE: Lodge has two meanings in Masonry. The first is the men or brethren who constitute the membership of the local fraternity. The second meaning is applied to the actual building where the brethren conduct their meetings. The building may also be called a Temple or a Hall or a Masonic Center.

LODGE ROOM: This is an open floor space within a Masonic building where the brethren conduct meetings and confer degrees on candidates.

OPERATIVE & SPECULATIVE MASONRY: Operative masons are the ones with chalk, charcoal, and clay on their hands. They are the workers who focus their attention on construction and architecture. Operative masonry predates Moses.

During the medieval times, workers formed into Guilds of tradesmen and craftsmen in order to exchange developments in the arts and sciences of their profession, to establish levels of proficiency, and to stabilize wages.

Speculative Masonry developed during the early Period of Enlightenment. It is often referred to as Symbolic Masonry because its uses the tools of Operative Masonry to inculcate moral, philosophical, and ethical truths and wisdom. The first recorded initiation of a non-operative mason was July 3, 1634, of the Right Honorable Lord Antoine Alexander in Edinburgh.

FREE & ACCEPTED: Many theories have been advanced as to the origin of the word "Free" within the word "Freemason". One theory relies on the fact that Speculative Masonic Lodges restricted their membership to men who were free, neither indentured nor enslaved.

A second theory is that it was used within Guilds to distinguish between two classes of Operative Masons: one being the hewers of stone blocks within quarries, the other being those who worked with the freed stones.

The third theory is that it was a corruption of the French phrase *frère maçon* or brother mason.

Three Letter and Four Letter Masons: In the 17th century, there was a rivalry in England between the two Grand Lodges. Eventually their differences were worked out, and they merged. By the time the union occurred, there were Grand Lodges in America that had received their Charters from the different Grand Lodges, and these 3-letter and 4-letter suffixes have remained in place.

> F.& A.M. is Free & Accepted Masons.
> A.F.& A.M. adds the word Ancient.
> A.F.M. in South Carolina is Ancient Free Masons.
> F.A.A.M. in Washington, D.C. is Free And Accepted Masons.

The bottom line is that the suffixes don't matter, and I have left these suffixes out of the text, except where absolutely necessary to explain an item of trivia.

BLUE LODGE or **CRAFT LODGE:** Masonic enlightenment is received by the candidate in progressive degrees, much as it was in the ancient craft lodges or guilds. Modern Freemasons are often referred to as Craftsmen. The color Blue is associated with these Lodges because of its historical symbolization of Truth and Fidelity.

There are three degrees that can be conferred on a candidate in a Blue Lodge.

Initiated an Entered Apprentice Mason,
Passed to the Degree of Fellowcraft Mason,
Raised to the Sublime Degree of Master Mason.

APPENDANT BODIES: A Master Mason has the option of petitioning to join other Masonic bodies. The most commonly joined bodies are York Rite Masonry, Scottish Rite Masonry, Shrine, and the coed Eastern Star. A Mason might belong to all or none of these.

York Rite has three separate bodies, the Chapter, the Council, and the Commandery. Their members are referred to as Royal Arch Companions, Cryptic and Select Companions, and Sir Knights of the Order of the Temple or Knights Templar.

American Blue Lodges, Royal Arch, and Cryptic Council accept men of any religious faith. The Knights Templar are Christians.

In the Capitular Degrees of Royal Arch Masonry, a Mason is:

Advanced to Mark Master,
Installed or Inducted a Virtual Past Master,
Received or Acknowledged a Most Excellent Master,
Exalted a Royal Arch Mason.

BIBLIOGRAPHY

Anderson, James, Dr., *Anderson's Constitutions of 1738*, The Masons Book Club, Bloomington, Illinois, 1978.

Brackett, Frank Parkhurst, *History of Pomona Valley, California: with biographical sketches*, Historic Record Company, Los Angeles, 1920.

Brown, William Adrian, *Facts, Fables, and Fantasies of Freemasonry*, History House Publications, Alexandria, Virginia, 1968.

Charles Clyde Hunt, *Masonic Symbolism*, Laurance Press Co., Cedar Rapids, 1939.

Coil, Henry Wilson, *Coil's Masonic Encyclopedia*, Macoy Publishing & Masonic Supply Company, New York, 1961.

Denslow, William R., *10,000 Famous Freemasons*, Vols 1-4, Missouri Lodge of Research, 1957.

Fairbrother, E.H., *A Masonic Anecdote*, Notes and Queries, Volume CLIX: 293-294, October, 25, 1930.

Frisbie, Granville Kimball, *Nuggets of Freemasonry In The Gold Rush Days of California*, Grand Lodge F. & A.M. of California, San Francisco, 1977.

Gibson, A. M., *The Life and Death of Colonel Albert Jennings Fountain*, University of Oklahoma Press, 1965.

Gillingham, Dennis, *Pioneer Masonry of the Golden State and other Historical Sketches*, Dennis Printers, Santa Ana, California, 1936.

Grand Lodge Committee on Masonic History, *One Hundred Years of Freemasonry in California, Vols 1-4*, Griffin Brothers, Inc., San Francisco, 1950.

Grand Lodge of New Zealand, *The New Zealand Freemason*, Vols: Spring, Summer, Winter, 1983.

Haywood, H.L., *Famous Masons and Masonic Presidents*, Masonic History Co., Illinois, 1948.

Johnston, Thomas, *The Old Masonic Lodge of Falkirk, now known as Lodge of St. John. No. 16*, Printed for the Lodge of Falkirk at the Herald Publishers Office, Falkirk, Scotland, 1887.

Langston, LaMoine, *A History of Masonry in New Mexico 1877-1977*, Poorbaugh Press, Roswell, 1977.

Leary, John J., Jr., *Talks With T.R., From the Diaries of John J. Leary, Jr.*, Houghton Mifflin Company, Boston and New York, 1920.

Mackey, Albert G. *A Text Book of Masonic Jurisprudence; Illustrating the Written and Unwritten Laws of Freemasonry*, Macoy & Sickels, Publishers, New York, 1864.

Mackey, Albert G., *A New and Revised Edition, An Encyclopedia of Freemasonry and Its Kindred Sciences*, The Masonic History Company, New York and London, 1914.

Mackey, Albert G., Dr., *Masonry Defined*, Masonic Supply Co., Memphis, 1930.

Mackey, Albert Gallatin, *The History of Freemasonry – The Legends of the Craft*, Barnes & Noble, New York, 1998.

Macoy, Robert, *A Dictionary of Freemasonry*, Gramercy Books, New York, 1989.

McKowen, Allister J., *Masonic Historiology*, Masonic Library of Southern California, October 8, 1946 – September 30, 1947.

Moore, Charles W., *Freemason's Monthly Magazine*, Vols 7-8, Tuttle &Dennett, Boston, 1848.

Oliver, Rev. George, *Book of the Lodge or Officer's Manual*, C.W. Oliver, Printer, Uppingham, 1849.

Peters, Madison C., *Masons as Makers of America*, Kessinger Publishing, Montana, 2003.

Recko, Corey, *Murder on the White Sands: The Disappearance of Albert and Henry Fountain*, University of North Texas Press, 2007.

Redding, M. Wolcott, *Masonic Antiquities of the Orient Unveiled*, Masonic Publishing Union, New York, 1878.

Roberts, Allen E., *House Undivided: The Story of Freemasonry and the Civil War*, Macoy Publishing & Masonic Supply Co., Inc., Richmond, Virginia, 1961.

Roberts, Allen E., *Masonic Trivia and Facts*, Anchor Communications, Highland Springs, Virginia, 1994.

Rubottom, Thomas W., *The Rubottom Family, Early Area Settlers*, Houston, Texas, 1976.

Shaver, William M., *Historical Sketch of the Cryptic Rite Pilgrimage to Colorado and Pike's Peak*, E.A. Armstrong Mfg. Co. , Chicago, 1900.

Sherman, Edwin A., editor, *Fifty Years of Masonry in California, Vols 1-2*, George Spaulding & Co., San Francisco, 1898.

Shuck, Oscar Tully, *Bench and bar in California: History, anecdotes, reminiscences By Oscar Tully Shuck*, The Occident Printing House, San Francisco, 1889.

Smythe, William E., *History of San Diego 1542-1908: An Account of the Rise and Progress of the Pioneer Settlement on the Pacific Coast of the United States, Volume II, The Modern City*, The History Company, San Diego, 1908.

Stansel, Edwin N., editor, *1850 – 1975 A History of Grand Lodge of Free and Accepted Masons State of California*, Grand Lodge of Free and Accepted Masons of the State of California, San Francisco, 1975.

Turnbull, Everett R., and Denslow, Ray V., *A History of Royal Arch Masonry, Vols 1-3*, Issued Under Authority of the General Grand Chapter Royal Arch Masons, 1956.

Waite, Arthur Edward, *A New Encyclopaedia of Freemasonry (Ars Magna Latomorum) and of Cognate Instituted Mysteries: Their Rites, Literature, and History*, Weathervance Books, New York, 1970.

Walkes, Joseph A., Jr., *Black Square and Compass: 200 Years of Prince-Hall Freemasonry*, Publishing & Masonic Supply Co., Inc., Richmond, Virginia, 1979.

Weston, R.C.G., *Centennial History N.Z. Pacific Lodge, No. 2 – 1842 -1942*, NZ Pacific Lodge No. 2, Wellington, 1942.

White, Elmer, *Knight Templary in the United States of America*, Phillips, Smyth & Van Orden and George Spaulding & Co., San Francisco, 1904.

Withee, John H., editor, *The Detroit Masonic News, Vol 2*, Detroit Masonic Temple Association, Detroit, 1921.

Wright, Dudley, editor, *Gould's History of Freemasonry Throughout the World, Revised, Vols 1-6*, Charles Scribner's Sons, New York, 1936.

_____, *American Architect and Building News*, Vol. LII, No. 1067, April-June 1896, Boston.

_____, *Army and Navy Journal*, March 5, 1864, New York City, New York.

_____, *Gardeners' Chronicles of American*, Vol. IX, No. 1, April 1909, National Association of Gardeners.

_____, *Imperial Valley Press*, Imperial Valley, California, 1908 -1910.

_____, *The American Tyler*, Vol. XVL, no.12; December 15, 1901, Ann Arbor, Michigan.

_____, *The Masonic Philatelist*, Vol. 44, No. 4., December 1988.

_____, *The Master Mason*, May 1925.

_____, *Wayne County Journal Banner*, Vol. 100, No. 22, July 15, 1976, Piedmont, Missouri.

INDEX

acacia 172
Acacia Lodge #15........................ 210
Akko Lodge #36 120
Al Malaikah Shrine 78
Albert J. Russell Lodge No. 12 54
alcohol.................................. 32, 164
Alexandria Lodge #22.................. 56
Alpha and Omega........................ 19
American Legion 127
Anchor Lodge #273 23
Annapolis Stone 154
Antarctica Lodge – No 777 52
Anti Masonic Party 161
Apopka, Florida 42
Argentina.................................... 178
Ashlar Lodge #91 124
Atascadero Lodge #493............... 66
Australia 36
Baraboo Lodge #34 70
Bazooka....................................... 29
Beaches Lodge #474................... 118
Belton Lodge #450 19
Benicia Lodge #5 .... 12, 175
Berkeley Lodge #33 102
Bermuda...................................... 16
Bible 180, 181
Boise Masonic Lodge #2.............. 67
bookplates................................... 174
Borglum....................................... 6
Boston Tea Party 49
Bowling Green Lodge #73 64
Brazil.. 143
Buchanan, James....................... 177
Caledonian Railway Masonic Lodge
    #354 83
California Lodge #1 147
California Lodge #13 11
Capital City Masonic Lodge #354 . 84
Capital Lodge #110....................... 19
Cariboo Lodge #469 58

Catalina Island Lodge #524 15
Centralia Chapter #44 202
Charleston Masonic Lodge #35...202
Chetek Lodge #227 65
Chukuni Lodge #660 40
Civil Service Lodge #148...............85
Clam Bake 43
Clay, Henry..................................192
Clear Lake Lodge #1417 206
Clinton, DeWitt 31
Concordia Lodge #50 19
Connecticut Lodge #75 12
Cooper, Rev. Canon William 16
cornerstone 23, 56, 130
Cowane, John..............................156
Craftsman Lodge #521 79
Crescent Lodge #133...................161
curling 5
Cuyahoga Falls Lodge #735...........67
Daintree Lodge #2938................117
Damascus Commandery #42 79
Davenport Lodge #37..................157
Dibble Lodge #109 19
Dillon Lodge #30 115
Doric Lodge 118
Doyle, Sir Arthur Canon 9
Dunedin Lodge #192 ....66, 67
E. Coppee MitchellMasonic Lodge
    #605..76
Eastgate Masonic Lodge 68
Eastland Lodge #467 115
Edward Dobbins Masonic Lodge
    #164..165
El Centro Lodge #384 116
Ellsworth Council #9 205
Esmeralda Lodge #6......................4
eunuchs......................................164
Evergreen Lodge #259 103
Farmers Lodge #168 65
Federal Lodge #1.....................26, 51

Fellowcraft, Names of twelve 27
Fidalgo Lodge #77 66
Ford, Gerald 178
Forest Lodge #130........................ 66
Forest Lodge #66..................... 171
Foshay Lodge #467 197
Franklin, Benjamin 107,173,207
Fredericksburg Lodge #4 101
Friendship Lodge #7 73
Garfield, James........................... 178
Germany 35
Girard, Stephen 105
Glasgow Star Lodge #219............... 3
Glittering Star Lodge #322 192
Golden Lodge #5 199
Golden Rule Lodge 118
Golden Rule Lodge #19 199
Gothic Lodge #270 148
Grand Hailing Sign....................... 35
Grand Orient of Egypt 8
Grand Orient of France 13,21
Granger Lodge #677................... 131
Grant, Ulysses 20
Grants Pass Lodge #84 67
Great Architect........................... 173
Greek Lodge 19
Guns N' Roses 156
Haiti... 186
Hampton Masonic Lodge 16
Hancock, John 189
Harding, Warren 176, 178
Harmony Lodge........................... 93
Hawaii 12, 158
Henrico Union Lodge #130........... 66
Heritage Lodge #730.................... 97
Highland Park Lodge #382 73
Hines, Edward 124
Hiram Abiff Boaz 131
Hiram Masonic Lodge #40 144
Hobo Degree 67
Hollenbeck Lodge #319............... 46
Hollywood Lodge #355 .....59, 66, 77
Household Brigade Lodge #2614 122
Howard Lodge #35 6
Huntington Beach Lodge #380..... 66
Invisible Lodge 86
Ione Lodge #80............................ 28
Ionic Lodge #474 15

Irish Military Lodge of Worcestershire
....192
Islands
  Clark's 200
  Freemason...............................37
  Masonic 38
Israel 12, 119, 197
It rains...5
Jackson, Andrew 177
James, Jesse 208
Jerusalem Lodge 123
Jerusalem Royal Arch Chapter #3 .72
Johnson, Andrew 177
Kane Lodge #454 ....19, 51
Kilwinning Lodge #356..........21, 146
King David's Lodge #209 ....,
.................................66, 150, 170
King George Lodge #59 65
King Solomon Territorial Lodge #592
King Solomon's Temple 30, 114
Kismet Temple Shrine...................51
Knights Templar 27
Knox Building 152
La Loge Française........................60
La Loge La Parfaite Union Lodge #17
....187
Lafayette 160
Lafayette Lodge #241 176
Lake Charles Lodge #16 46
Lake Erie Lodge #347 74
Laughlin, Nevada 204
Laurens, Henry...........................190
Lawrence Lodge # 6 175
Le Progres de L'Oceanie #124.....194
Lee Lodge #209 ....24, 33
Letter of Marque 129
license plates 18
Lincoln Park Lodge 159
Lincoln, Abraham 142
Lively Stone Lodge #22 199
Lodge #239 of Paris, France........191
Lodge Jamrud #4372...................198
Lodge of Regeneration, Portugal 205
Lodge St. George #200.................17
Los Angeles Lodge #42.................88
Maiden Lodge No. 692.................54
Mallet and Chisel Lecture 9
Mammoth Cave 196

Mariposa Lodge #23 126
Martin's Station Lodge #188 196
Martini 14
Matinecock Lodge #806 183
McKinley, William 178
Mecca Shrine 79
Mencius 28
Merrickville Masonic Lodge #55 105
Mexico 186
Mickey Mouse 20
Miles Lodge #341 64
Mission Bay Lodge #771 195
Modesto Masonic Lodge #206 14
Morgan Park Lodge #999 63
Morning Star Lodge #159 75
Morton, William 157
Moslem Shrine Temple 79
Mother Tucker's Restaurant 158
Motorcycle Association 67
Mount Hermon Lodge #118 24
Mount Moriah Lodge #4 6
Mount Moriah Lodge #44 13
Mt. Carmel Lodge #133 67
Mt. Moriah Lodge #59 140
Mt. Moriah Lodge #40 153
Musicians Lodge #2881 84
Mystic Brotherhood Lodge #21,. 107
Mythbusters 48
Napoleon 13, 128
Nation Lodge #566 198
Navy Lodge #2612 122
Norseman Lodge #878 51
Northfield, Minnesota 208
Nudism 4
Oakland Lodge #188 127
oath 33, 34, 180, 181
Oceanside-San Dieguito Lodge #381
.... 170
Official Clock Winder 16
Old Denstonian Lodge #5490 131
Old Ironsides 198
Oleeta Lodge No. 145 54
Oneida Chapter #57 203
onion 33
Operative Lodge #150 82
Operative Lodge #40 82
Orient Lodge #395 66
Oriental Lodge #500 112
Overseas Lodge #40 85

Pacific Lodge 175
Pacific Lodge #233 79
Palestine Lodge #357 15
Palmer Lodge #372 201
Parthenon Lodge #1101 19
Pencil 20
Penrhyn Lodge #258 83
Philanthropic Lodge #304 7
Pike, Albert 158
Pleasant Grove Lodge #22 64
Pledge of Allegiance 9
Poinsett, Dr. Joel 167
Polk, James 177
Pomona Lodge #246 89
Potato 23
Potunk Lodge #1071 4
Prairieville "Poetry" Lodge #253 ... 64
Probity Lodge #61 58
Pyramid, Dorn 150
Quitman Lodge #96 147
Randolph, Peyton 189
Reagan, Ronald 188
Recovery Lodge #31 167
Red House 10
Richard Vaux Lodge #384 72
Ridgefield Daylight Lodge #237 66
Riverside Chapter #67 203
Robert Burns Masonic Lodge #97
.... 195
Rockton Lodge #316 152
Roof of the World Masonic Lodge
#1094 202
Roosevelt, Franklin 178
Roosevelt, Theodore 130, 183
Gardner 183
Royal Arch Masons Monroe Chapter
#1 79
Royal White Hart Lodge #2 40
Russia 25
Rutland Lodge #298 65
S.W. Hackett Lodge #574 66
Santa Anna, General 167
Santa Cruz Lodge #38 161
Sarasota Lodge #417 74
Science Lodge #50 125
Shade Lodge #18 147
Shakespeare 34
Shakespeare Lodge #750 4

Silentia Lodge #198 186
Sketchley, James 130
Skykomish Lodge #259 65
Society of Blue Friars.................. 86
Södermanland............................ 24
Sojourners Lodge, Panama 120
Soliman, Angelo 98
Solomon Lodge #20 81
Solomons Lodge #1 167
Somerset Lodge #34 186
Somerville Lodge #451.............. 121
Southern California Masonic Lodge
    #529 66
SS President Hoover.................. 102
St. Clair, General Arthur 190
St. George's Lodge #6 122
St. John's Lodge #1.................... 180
St. John's Lodge #73.................... 13
St. Johns Lodge #36...................... 60
St. Louis Lodge #86 175
St. Paul's Lodge 131
stamps..................31, 117, 138, 160
steam powered typewriter 23
Submarine, Hunley..................... 139
Sunset Chapter #23.................... 202
Sutherland Lodge #174 67
Sutter Lodge #6 12
Sweden 24
Taft, William Howard 146
Tandragee Lodge #79.................. 37
Temple Lodge #296..................... 97
Thomas, Danny 148
Tillamook Rock Lighthouse 101
Time Immemorial........................ 25
Toping 22
Tranquility Lodge 206
Treadwell Lodge #213................. 40
Trenton Masonic Temple 209
True Harmony 99

True Harmony Lodge 113
Truman, Harry...................... 19, 178
Tuscan Lodge #44 38
Union Lodge #38.........................194
Union Lodge #58..........................43
Union Lodge #593........................65
University Lodge #394 78
US Senate...................................192
USS *Maine*................................40
Utopia Lodge #527......................80
Utopia Lodge #537......................77
Van Buren Lodge #6......................29
Varick Lodge #31..........................22
Vincennes Lodge # 1 78
Volcano Lodge #56 194
Vonore Lodge #658....................195
Waco Lodge #92 60
Washington, George.........................
    ....32, 100, 180, 185
wedding 21
West Roxbury Lodge....................54
Western Star #98 12
Westhope Lodge #74 38
What Cheer Lodge 108
Whatcom Lodge #151................102
Wheeler, Henry..........................208
Whicher, John 170
Winchester Hiram Masonic Lodge
    #24..42
Winnedumah Lodge #287..........192
Winter Park Lodge #239 67
Wirt, William..............................161
Women Masons..........................166
Worshipful 41
Wyandotte Lodge #3 61
Zekekiah's Cave 195
Zetland Lodge #852 131
Zion Lodge #77............................15

ABOUT THE AUTHOR

Peter Champion has a wry sense of humor and a love of puns, much to the consternation of friends and family. His mother, Huldah, believed it developed because God had a tickle in his nose and sneezed at the moment of Peter's birth.

His diverse background includes time in the South Pacific as a merchant seaman, a professional actor, an elementary school classroom teacher, a junior high school industrial arts instructor, manager of an Italian restaurant, and an operator of commercial apiaries.

He has been a Freemason since 1972 and had the privilege of serving as Worshipful Master of King David's Lodge #209, in San Luis Obispo. He is an officer in the San Luis Royal Arch Chapter #62, San Luis Obispo Cryptic Council #38, Knights Templar Commandery #27, and Channel Coast Council #114 of Allied Masonic Degrees. He is a member of several Masonic organizations in Southern California, including; Al Malaikah Shrine in Los Angeles, Brian Boru Council #38 Knight Masons in Long Beach, Southern California Research Lodge, and Santa Barbara Scottish Rite.

He is the author of the informative and entertaining:
San Luis Obispo Freemasonry 1860 - 2013

20027100R00132

Printed in Poland
by Amazon Fulfillment
Poland Sp. z o.o., Wrocław